LIGHT & SIMPLE COOKING YEAR-ROUND

SOUTHWESTERN

GRILLING

LIGHT & SIMPLE COOKING YEAR-ROUND
SOUTHWESTERN GRILLING

JANE STACEY

PHOTOGRAPHY BY
ANN STRATTON

BROADWAY BOOKS   NEW YORK

S O U T H W E S T E R N   G R I L L I N G

Copyright © 1997 by Smallwood and Stewart. All rights reserved. Printed in
Singapore. No part of this book may be reproduced or transmitted in any form
or by any means, electronic or mechanical, including photocopying, recording,
or by any information storage and retrieval system, without written permission from the
publisher. For information, address Broadway Books, a division of Bantam
Doubleday Dell Publishing Group, Inc., 1540 Broadway, New York, NY 10036.

Broadway Books titles may be purchased for business or promotional use or for special sales.
For information, please write to: Special Markets Department, Bantam
Doubleday Dell Publishing Group, Inc., 1540 Broadway, New York, NY 10036.

BROADWAY BOOKS and its logo, a letter B bisected on the diagonal,
are trademarks of Broadway Books, a division of Bantam Doubleday Dell Publishing Group, Inc.

Library of Congress Cataloging-in-Publication Data

Stacey, Jane.
Southwestern grilling: light and simple cooking year-round / Jane Stacey.—1st ed.
p. cm.
ISBN 0-553-06166-6 (pbk.)
1. Barbecue cookery. 2. Cookery, American—Southwestern style. I. Title.
TX840.88S72 1997 96-53568
641.7′6—DC21 CIP

FIRST EDITION
Produced by Smallwood and Stewart, Inc., New York

Edited by: Deborah Mintcheff
Designed by: Susi Oberhelman
Food Stylist: Rori Spinelli
Prop Stylist: Denise Canter

ISBN 0-553-06166-6

97 98 99 00 01 10 9 8 7 6 5 4 3 2 1

CONTENTS

INTRODUCTION

G O N E   A R E   T H E   D A Y S   when grilling meant only thick slabs of T-bone steak or sauce-laden racks of ribs. Our growing consciousness about healthful eating and our appreciation of other cuisines have spawned an explosion of a new kind of cooking much of which is particularly well suited to grilling. Today, for example, we are using lean, thinner cuts of meat, poultry, and fish that cook quickly, and often serving vegetables, and even salads, as main dishes.

The Southwest's unique array of seasonings and ingredients is ideally suited for grilled foods. Chiles, fresh or dried, grilled or roasted, offer a whole world of flavors that are often more pronounced than their heat, adding character to simple grilled foods. To contrast with the warm, dark accents of chiles, Southwestern cooking often uses the bright, clean taste of lime juice both to flavor and tenderize food. Cumin, cilantro, and other herbs and spices contribute additional flavors. Salsas, in their colorful and seemingly endless variety, accentuate the freshness of grilled poultry, fish, and meat. What was once an occasional summertime ritual has for many become a year-round celebration.

TYPES OF GRILLS

Aside from size (which determines how much food can be cooked at one time), the most important variable when choosing a grill is the gauge of the metal. Heavier, thicker steel will hold and conduct heat more evenly and longer than thinner metals, and it's more durable as well. Compare the sturdiness of various grill grates in particular. Most grills have lids or hoods that make it possible to grill larger items by containing some of the moisture and heat. Large roasts, turkey, and other large birds require a rotisserie, which is electrically operated.

GAS GRILLS   Using a gas grill is by far the easiest and fastest way to grill. Gas grills eliminate much of the guesswork about temperature, since most can be set simply by the turn of a knob to produce a range of heat from low to high. These grills use either propane gas, which comes in tanks (5-gallon tanks are the most common and will last for about 5 hours), or natural gas, which requires a special hook-up to your gas line. Either way, the gas heats a bed of ceramic briquettes or lava stones that radiate heat, cooking the food. Hardwood smoking chips (dry or soaked in water), woody stalks of dried herbs, or even chunks of hardwood can be added to enhance flavor. Some cooks claim the flavor produced by gas grilling is inferior to that of food grilled over wood or charcoal, but I think that the convenience and ease of controlling the heat outweighs this possible drawback. (I do use a small, portable charcoal grill, especially for picnics.)

A gas grill requires 20 to 30 minutes to preheat, and it is easy to clean with a sturdy wire brush.

Both for health purposes and to prevent food from sticking, always keep the grates clean; brush them lightly with oil before grilling. Grilling with gas does not require the constant attention to the fire that cooking with charcoal does, but always use caution. Read and follow the manufacturer's recommendations for lighting the grill and cooking.

CHARCOAL GRILLS   Charcoal grills come in a wide variety of sizes and shapes. Some of the most popular styles are:

Braziers — A brazier is nothing more than a firebox on legs. Braziers vary in shape and size. Some have hoods and adjustable air vents and some can be upscaled with rotisserie attachments. They are all designed for cooking with direct heat.

Hibachis — These small rectangular grills, with deep narrow fireboxes for fuel efficiency, were first used in Japan. Hibachis do not have covers and are meant for direct-heat cooking only. They work best for small foods that cook quickly, such as kebabs, shrimp, or thin fish fillets.

Kettle grills — These lidded grills are made for covered and uncovered cooking, as well as grilling over indirect heat. The cover gives you more control over the grilling process, allowing you to maintain a more even temperature, keep moisture in, and reduce flare-ups. To control the heat, there are adjustable air-vents in the cover and under the rack that holds the charcoal; when they are open, the increased airflow fans the fire and produces more heat. Kettle grills can also be outfitted with electric rotisseries.

TYPES OF FUELS

There are two main types of charcoal: charcoal briquettes and hardwood (lump) charcoal.

Charcoal briquettes — Briquettes are made from wood scraps and/or coal smoldered into carbon, mixed with a filler, and pressed into briquettes. Look at the list of ingredients on the bag before you choose your briquettes. Many brands contain petroleum products and chemical additives that may be questionable healthwise and may impart an unwanted flavor to the food.

Hardwood charcoal — Hardwood charcoal is made from charred wood. It does not have the uniform shape of briquettes and doesn't contain additives and fillers. It burns hotter, cleaner, and more efficiently than charcoal briquettes, and some cooks claim it produces a better flavor as well. Unfortunately, hardwood charcoal is not always readily available and is more expensive than charcoal briquettes.

LIGHTING CHARCOAL The easiest and perhaps the most common way to start a charcoal fire is to use a liquid fire starter. However, these starters contain petroleum products that must be allowed to burn off completely before beginning to cook so the food is not flavored with their residues.

I prefer to use a chimney starter, a heavy metal cylinder with a metal grate toward the bottom of the cylinder. To use a chimney starter, loosely crumple some newspaper and stuff it under the grate.

Place the chimney on the fuel bed or directly in the firebox. Pile the charcoal inside the chimney and use a match to ignite the paper. Wait until you are sure the coals have ignited (five to ten minutes) before upending the coals into the firebox.

You can also use an electric starter, a long handled heating element that heats the coals it touches until they ignite. However, it requires a nearby outlet and some of the coals can remain unlit. Paraffin-soaked starter blocks are simply placed among the coals and lit with a match. Because they contain highly-flammable paraffin, they ignite quickly and easily. Starter bags are bags of charcoal briquettes that are placed directly in the firebox. You light the whole bag with a match and then spread the coals once they are ignited. I avoid them both because they are expensive and because they contain petroleum products and chemical additives that may flavor the food.

The amount of coals you need depends on the kind and amount of food you are grilling. A good rule of thumb is to create a bed of coals (I prefer a double layer) that will extend about an inch beyond the area taken up by the food.

It usually takes about 30 minutes to get a charcoal fire ready for cooking. The coals should develop a layer of gray ash covering their red glow and you should be able to hold your hand 3 inches above the coals for no more than 3 to 5 seconds.

GRILLING ADVICE

Though the recipes in this book give guidelines for how much heat to use and for cooking times, be sure to watch your food carefully as it cooks. If the food is beginning to burn, reduce the heat by raking some of the hot coals to the side, moving the food away from the hottest part of the fire, or reducing the gas flame. (As a last resort, keep a spray bottle of water available to douse flames and flare-ups.)

Most foods are grilled directly over coals. When grilling roasts, whole chickens, hams, turkeys, and pizzas, you will need to cook using indirect heat with the grill cover in place. The individual recipes specify when to use indirect heat and how to create it. Keep in mind that removing the grill cover to check the food allows the heat to escape and may affect cooking times, especially for large items.

High winds or extremely cold weather also affect grilling times. Choose a sheltered spot for your grill, a place that is out of the wind yet provides ample clearance from walls, roof overhangs, and bushes.

Grilling cooks food at high temperatures — at least 400°F to 600°F — so it is very important to use sturdy long-handled utensils and heavy mitts. Keep a long-handled heatproof brush for oiling the grill grates. It is also wise to have all your grilling tools assembled at the grill when you are ready to cook — that way, you never have to leave the grill unattended. Be especially careful to keep children at a safe distance from the grill.

Whatever type of grill or fuel you use, remember that grilling is a cooking technique refined by knowledge, practice, and a sense of humor. I hope you will discover new and inspiring ideas in this collection of recipes you can incorporate into your own personal grilling style.

APPETIZERS & SOUPS

TOMATO SOUP

SMOKY

The rich dark flavor of this soup comes from the combination of grilled ripe tomatoes and red bell pepper, with a hint of red wine. Just barely cooking the soup keeps the flavors fresh.

Serves 4

PREHEAT THE GRILL to medium and brush with oil. Soak four 6- to 8-inch bamboo skewers in cold water for at least 30 minutes.

In a large bowl, combine the tomatoes, bell pepper, onion, 1 tablespoon of the oil, and the cumin. Toss, season with salt and pepper, and toss again.

Grill the vegetables, turning them, for 5 to 7 minutes, or until the tomato skins are blistered and brown, the pepper is softened, and the onion is tender. Remove and set aside.

In a small skillet, heat the remaining 1 tablespoon oil over medium heat. Add the garlic and cook, for about 1 minute. Add the red wine and transfer to a food processor.

Add the grilled vegetables and crushed tomatoes to the food processor; process until smooth. Press the vegetables through a food mill into a large saucepan. Add the broth and bring to a simmer over medium heat. Season with salt and pepper and keep warm.

Meanwhile, in a medium-size bowl, combine the shrimp, vinegar, and chile powder and toss until the shrimp are evenly coated. Thread the shrimp onto the skewers. Grill for 2 to 3 minutes on each side, or until the shrimp are bright pink and firm to the touch.

To serve, ladle the soup into bowls, place a shrimp skewer on each rim, and garnish with a spoonful of sour cream.

Ingredients

- 10 plum tomatoes, halved
- 1 medium-size red bell pepper, halved, cored & seeded
- ½ medium-size onion
- 2 tablespoons olive oil
- ¾ teaspoon ground cumin
- Salt & freshly ground pepper
- 2 garlic cloves, minced
- ½ cup dry red wine
- 2 cups canned crushed tomatoes
- 3 cups vegetable or chicken broth
- 12 large shrimp (about ½ pound), peeled & deveined
- 2 tablespoons cider vinegar
- 1 teaspoon medium-hot pure chile powder
- Low-fat sour cream, for garnish

EGGPLANT SOUP

ROASTED

I once worked at an Italian restaurant that served an exquisite creamy eggplant soup. This variation adds the nutty, sweet flavor of roasted garlic and the distinctly Southwestern flavor of cumin. Fresh lemon juice, stirred in just before serving, brightens all the flavors.

Serves 4

P REHEAT THE GRILL to medium and brush with oil.

Grill the eggplants and onion, turning often, for 6 to 8 minutes, or until the eggplant is blackened and soft and the onion is soft. Remove from the grill and set aside until cool enough to handle.

Peel the eggplants and cut into coarse chunks. In a food processor or blender, process the eggplant, onion, and garlic, in batches, until completely smooth. Transfer the mixture to a large saucepan and stir in the broth, cumin, salt, and pepper.

Bring to a simmer and cook, stirring occasionally, for 10 minutes. Remove from the heat and stir in the lemon juice. Ladle the soup into warm soup bowls, garnish with parsley, and serve.

2 medium-size eggplants (about 1 pound each)

1 medium-size onion, quartered

1 head roasted garlic*, peeled

4 cups chicken broth

¾ teaspoon ground cumin

½ teaspoon salt

¼ teaspoon freshly ground pepper

2 tablespoons fresh lemon juice

Chopped fresh parsley, for garnish

*ROASTED GARLIC Preheat the oven to 375°F. Put the garlic into a small oven-proof dish and drizzle with 2 tablespoons olive oil. Cover with foil and bake for about 45 minutes, or until softened.

SWEET CORN &

Serves 4 to 6

This soup is deliciously sweet, with the full flavor of roasted corn in every spoonful. The secret is to simmer the corn cobs right along with the corn and broth. The cobs are then discarded and the soup pureed.

PREHEAT THE GRILL to medium and brush with oil.

Grill the corn, turning often, for 6 to 8 minutes, or until lightly browned on all sides. Remove from the grill and set aside until cool enough to handle.

In a large saucepan, melt the butter over medium heat. Add the onion and cook, stirring, for 2 to 3 minutes, or until soft and translucent. Remove from the heat.

Use a sharp knife to cut the corn from the cobs and add the corn to the saucepan. Use a large knife or cleaver to cut the corn cobs in half and add to the pan. Stir in 4 cups of the broth and bring to a boil over medium-high heat. Reduce the heat to low and simmer, covered, for 25 minutes. Using tongs, remove and discard the corn cobs.

In a food processor, blender, or food mill, process the soup, in batches, until smooth and return to the saucepan. Stir in the half-and-half and the remaining 2 cups broth. Bring to a simmer over low heat and season with salt and pepper. Ladle into warm soup bowls and garnish with dots or swirls of Sriracha sauce.

6 ears fresh corn, husks & silk removed

2 tablespoons butter

½ medium-size onion, chopped

6 cups chicken broth

½ cup half-and-half

Salt & freshly ground pepper

Sriracha hot chile sauce*

*Sriracha sauce is a Thai-style hot chile sauce made from serrano chiles, vinegar, garlic, and salt. It is available in Asian food stores.

JACK PIZZA

I find that this pizza dough recipe makes perfect pizzas. The crispy cracker-like crust can only be achieved by using a very stiff dough. Simple toppings such as Monterey jack cheese and tomatoes make for easy preparation and elegant finger food.

Serves 4

PUT THE WATER AND YEAST into a large bowl and stir until the yeast has dissolved. Let stand for 5 minutes, or until bubbly. Stir in the oil, honey, 2¾ cups of the all-purpose flour, the semolina flour, and salt, stirring until a stiff dough forms.

Turn the dough onto a floured work surface and knead for 8 minutes, or until smooth, sprinkling with additional flour if needed. Put the dough into a large oiled bowl, turning to coat. Cover and set aside in a warm place for about 1 hour, or until doubled in volume.

Preheat the grill to medium and brush with oil.

Punch down the dough and turn onto a floured work surface. Divide into 3 pieces. Wrap and freeze two pieces of the dough. Shape the remaining piece of dough into a ball. Roll out on the floured surface into a free-form round approximately 9 inches in diameter.

Prepare the grill for indirect grilling: Turn off one side of the grill if using a two burner gas grill. If using a charcoal grill, rake the hot coals to one side. Place the dough on the hot side, cover, and grill for barely 1 minute, or until puffed and grill-marked. Turn the crust over and transfer to a work surface. (If you are using a single-burner gas grill, place the pizza dough on the grill for slightly less than 1 minute, then reduce the heat to low before putting the pizza back onto the grill.)

Sprinkle the cheese over the crust and top with the tomatoes and jalapeño. Slide the pizza back onto the cool side of the grill. Cover and grill for 5 minutes, or until the cheese has melted and the crust is browned. Cut into wedges, and serve.

PIZZA DOUGH

1 cup warm water (105°F to 115°F)

1 package active dry yeast

2 tablespoons olive oil

1 tablespoon honey

2¾ to 3 cups all-purpose flour

1 cup semolina flour

½ teaspoon salt

¾ cup grated Monterey Jack or Pepper Jack cheese

2 plum tomatoes, chopped

1 jalapeño chile, seeded & finely chopped

SIMPLE QUESADILLAS

These days quesadillas have gone upscale, containing ingredients such as smoked duck, goat cheese, and lobster. I still like the simplest quesadillas the best. Nothing can beat the flavor of fresh flour tortillas folded around Monterey Jack or Cheddar cheese and jalapeño chiles. Grilled just long enough to melt the cheese and toast the tortillas, these quesadillas are sheer perfection.

Serves 4

PREHEAT THE GRILL to medium and brush with oil.

Place the tortillas on a work surface. Sprinkle ½ cup of the cheese on the bottom half of each tortilla and top the cheese with the jalapeños. Gently fold the unfilled half of the tortillas over the cheese, pressing lightly to compress the filling.

Grill the quesadillas, turning once, for about 2 minutes, or until nicely marked and lightly browned. Cut each quesadilla into 3 wedges, place on a small platter, and serve.

4 large flour tortillas (8 to 10 inches in diameter)

2 cups grated Monterey Jack or mild Cheddar cheese (8 ounces)

½ cup pickled jalapeño slices or 4 fresh jalapeño chiles, thinly sliced

Serves 4 to 6

Here, the dark earthy taste of the roasted poblano chile is accented by the sweet flavor of grilled eggplant. Poblanos rank rather low on the heat scale, making them a natural choice if you are not accustomed to eating chiles.

PREHEAT THE GRILL to medium and brush with oil.

Toast the sesame seeds in a small skillet over medium heat, shaking the pan occasionally, for 1 to 2 minutes, or until golden brown and fragrant. Transfer to a small dish and set aside.

Grill the eggplant for 6 to 8 minutes, or until the skin is blackened and the eggplant is soft. Set aside until cool enough to handle.

Grill the chile, turning often, for 3 to 4 minutes, or until the skin is blistered and brown. Wrap the chile in a paper towel, seal tightly in a plastic bag, and steam for 10 minutes. Remove the chile and let cool, then peel, core, and seed. Cut the chile into ¼-inch dice. Set aside.

Peel the eggplant and cut into coarse chunks. In a food processor or blender, combine the eggplant, garlic, cumin, salt, and sesame seeds and process until smooth. Transfer the eggplant mixture to a serving dish and stir in the poblano chile. Set aside.

Brush both sides of the bread slices with oil and sprinkle lightly on one side with kosher salt. Grill for about 10 to 15 seconds on each side, or until golden. Serve the eggplant caviar accompanied by the warm grilled toasts.

EGGPLANT CAVIAR

1 tablespoon sesame seeds

1 medium-size eggplant (about 1 pound)

1 poblano chile

½ head roasted garlic (about 8 cloves) (page 16), peeled

½ teaspoon ground cumin

¼ teaspoon salt

GRILLED TOASTS

Approximately eighteen ¼-inch-thick slices French bread

Olive oil for brushing

Kosher salt for sprinkling

MARINATED GOAT CHEESE

Here, fresh goat cheese is marinated in olive oil, cumin, and green olives. Grilled French bread toasts are spread with roasted garlic and then topped with slices of the marinated cheese. The fresh cilantro then brightens the flavors, making this an appetizer you will want to prepare time and again.

Serves 6 to 8

Prepare the green olive marinade: Toast the cumin seeds in a small skillet over medium-low heat for about 2 minutes, or until fragrant. Transfer to a small bowl.

Whisk in the oil, vinegar, salt, and pepper until blended. Stir in the olives. Put the cheese in a shallow dish and pour the marinade over. Cover with plastic wrap and marinate in the refrigerator for at least 1 or up to 3 hours.

Preheat the grill to medium and brush with oil.

Lightly brush both sides of the bread slices with oil and sprinkle lightly on one side with kosher salt. Grill for 10 to 15 seconds on each side, or until golden. Remove and keep warm.

To serve, remove the cheese to a serving platter. Cut off the top of the garlic heads, exposing the garlic pulp. Remove 4 of the garlic cloves and gently squeeze out the pulp. Use a fork to mash the garlic, then stir into the marinade. Place the heads of roasted garlic in the center of the platter, drizzle the marinade over the cheese, and sprinkle with the chopped cilantro. Arrange the toasts on the platter and serve.

GREEN OLIVE MARINADE

- 1 teaspoon cumin seeds
- 3 tablespoons extra-virgin olive oil
- 3 tablespoons white wine vinegar
- 1/4 teaspoon salt
- 1/4 teaspoon freshly ground pepper
- 1/4 cup coarsely chopped pitted Spanish green olives

- 3 fresh goat cheese logs, such as Montrachet (5 ounces each), at room temperature
- Twenty-four 1/4-inch-thick-slices French bread
- Olive oil
- Kosher salt
- 2 large heads roasted garlic (page 16), peeled
- 1 tablespoon coarsely chopped fresh cilantro

POBLANOS

Serves 6 to 8

This recipe was inspired in part by my friend Dodie, who suggested adding toasted pine nuts and feta cheese to the grilled vegetable filling. She was, and usually is, right. The pine nuts add richness, the feta cheese just a touch of creaminess and a tang. These stuffed poblanos also make an unusual side dish or light vegetarian main dish.

PREHEAT THE GRILL to medium and brush with oil.

Grill the chiles, turning several times, for 3 to 4 minutes, or until the skins are blistered and brown. Wrap the chiles in paper towels, seal in a plastic bag, and let steam for 10 minutes. Remove and let cool. Meanwhile, grill the corn, turning it, for 5 to 6 minutes, or until browned in spots. Grill the squash for about 1 minute on each side, or until grill-marked but still firm. Remove from the grill.

Preheat the oven to 375°F.

Cut the corn from the cob and cut the squash into ½-inch wide pieces. Put into a medium-size bowl, along with the pine nuts, scallion, cilantro, parsley, and garlic, tossing to combine. Add the feta cheese, season with salt and pepper, and toss.

Carefully peel and core the chiles, then cut lengthwise in half and remove the seeds. Spoon 2 tablespoons of the corn mixture into the center of a chile half. Fold the ends of the chile over the filling, overlapping them, and secure with toothpicks. Put the chile into a shallow baking dish or pie plate and continue to fill the remaining chiles.

Bake, uncovered, for 12 to 15 minutes, or until sizzling hot. Serve, passing the hot sauce on the side, if desired.

5 poblano chiles

1 ear fresh corn, husk & silk removed

1 small yellow squash, cut lengthwise into ¼-inch-thick slices

2 tablespoons pine nuts, toasted

1 scallion, finely chopped

1 tablespoon chopped fresh cilantro

1 tablespoon chopped fresh parsley

1 garlic clove, minced

½ cup crumbled feta cheese

Salt & freshly ground pepper

Hot sauce, for serving

Serves 4 to 6

REHEAT THE GRILL to medium and brush with oil.

Place the mussels and clams directly on the grill and grill for 2 to 4 minutes, or until the shells open. Remove the mussels and clams as they open to a platter discarding any that do not, and let cool slightly. Pull off half of each mussel and clam shell, discarding the empty half-shells. Place the mussels and clams, in their shells, on a warm serving platter. Top each with about ¼ teaspoon cilantro pesto and serve immediately.

Since I live so far from the ocean, I really appreciate the increasing availability of fresh seafood throughout the country. Clams and mussels are always a treat, especially when grilled and topped with cilantro pesto. Placed directly on the grill, mussels and clams steam in their own clean-tasting briny juices. The combination of the shellfish and the freshly prepared pesto will transport you right back to your favorite beach.

1 pound mussels, scrubbed
  & debearded

1 pound littleneck clams,
  scrubbed

About ½ cup Cilantro Pesto*

*Cilantro Pesto
In a food processor, combine 1½ cups each loosely packed fresh cilantro and parsley leaves, 1 jalapeño chile, seeded and ribs removed, and 1 garlic clove. Pulse twice, or until coarsely chopped. With the machine running, add ½ cup olive oil, in a steady stream, processing until smooth. Transfer the pesto to a small serving bowl, and stir in 1 tablespoon fresh lemon juice and ¼ teaspoon salt.

CILANTRO PESTO

FIERY RÉMOULADE

A touch of mild red chile powder, a sprinkling of parsley, and a spoonful of chopped capers transform ordinary mayonnaise into an elegant dipping sauce for grilled skewered vegetables.

Serves 4 to 6

PREHEAT THE GRILL to medium and brush with oil. Soak twelve 8- to 10-inch bamboo skewers in cold water for at least 30 minutes.

Prepare the red chile rémoulade: In a small bowl, mix together all the rémoulade ingredients until well combined. Cover and refrigerate until ready to use.

In a large bowl, combine the mushrooms, bell peppers, squash, tomatoes, and eggplant. In a small bowl, whisk the oil, lemon juice, and chile rub together. Drizzle over the vegetables and toss until evenly coated. Thread the vegetables onto the skewers, dividing them evenly.

Grill the vegetables, turning them often, for 6 to 8 minutes, or until grill-marked and tender but not soft. Place the vegetable skewers on a platter and serve accompanied by the rémoulade.

RED CHILE RÉMOULADE

- 1¼ cups good-quality mayonnaise
- 3 tablespoons fresh lemon juice
- 3 tablespoons olive oil
- 1 tablespoon chopped fresh cilantro
- 1 tablespoon chopped fresh parsley
- 2 teaspoons adobo sauce (from canned chipotle chiles)
- 2 teaspoons capers, chopped
- 1 teaspoon mild pure chile powder
- ¼ teaspoon freshly ground pepper

- 8 ounces button mushrooms, stems trimmed & briefly rinsed
- 1 each medium-size red & green bell pepper, halved, cored, seeded & cut into 1-inch chunks
- 1 small yellow squash, halved lengthwise & cut crosswise into ¼-inch-thick slices
- 2 plum tomatoes, halved & cut crosswise into ½-inch-thick slices
- 1 small Japanese eggplant, halved lengthwise & cut crosswise into ¼-inch-thick slices
- 2 tablespoons olive oil
- 2 tablespoons fresh lemon juice
- 1 teaspoon Red Chile Rub (page 106)

THE MAIN COURSE

TOMATILLO SALSA

Tomatillos resemble small green tomatoes covered with a papery skin. They have a unique citrus flavor and are used both raw and cooked in salsas and sauces. Canned tomatillos can be used for other sauces, but I do not recommend them for this salsa. Only the bright taste of fresh tomatillos will stand up to the flavor of the lemony chicken.

Serves 4

ON A WORK SURFACE, place each chicken breast between 2 pieces of plastic wrap and pound to a uniform thickness. Sprinkle the chicken lightly with salt and put into a shallow baking dish.

Prepare the lemon marinade: In a small bowl, whisk all the marinade ingredients together. Pour over the chicken, turning to coat evenly. Cover and marinate in the refrigerator for at least 2 or up to 6 hours.

Preheat the grill to medium and brush with oil.

Prepare the tomatillo salsa: In a food processor, combine all the salsa ingredients. Pulse until the mixture forms a chunky puree. Transfer the salsa to a serving dish, cover, and refrigerate until ready to serve.

Grill the chicken breasts for 4 to 5 minutes on each side, or until nicely marked and cooked through. Remove to a platter and serve accompanied by the tomatillo salsa.

4 boneless skinless chicken breast halves (5 to 6 ounces each)

Salt

LEMON MARINADE

1 cup fresh lemon juice

⅓ cup chopped fresh cilantro

⅓ cup chopped fresh parsley

2 tablespoons peanut or vegetable oil

3 garlic cloves, thinly sliced

1 imported bay leaf

TOMATILLO SALSA

8 to 9 fresh tomatillos, papery skin removed & rinsed

4 garlic cloves

2 jalapeño chiles, seeded & ribs removed

2 scallions, coarsely chopped

½ cup loosely packed fresh cilantro leaves

½ cup loosely packed fresh parsley leaves

¼ cup plus 2 tablespoons fresh lime juice

1 teaspoon honey

¼ teaspoon salt

BBQ CHICKEN

Serves 4

I often find that barbecue sauces are too sweet. This Southwest-inspired recipe contains beer, cumin, and pure red chile powder, which gives the sauce depth of flavor and just the right amount of heat. The chicken is first baked and then grilled, which ensures that it will be cooked to perfection without the sauce burning.

PREPARE THE BARBECUE SAUCE: In a large saucepan, heat the oil over medium heat. Add the onions and garlic and cook, stirring, for 2 to 3 minutes. Add the beer, vinegar, and bay leaves and cook for about 3 minutes, or until the liquid is slightly reduced. Add the remaining marinade ingredients. Reduce the heat and simmer, stirring, for 10 minutes, or until slightly thickened. Remove and cool.

Preheat the oven to 325°F.

Put the chicken into a baking dish and cover with 1 cup of the barbecue sauce.

Bake the chicken, skin side up, for 30 minutes, or just until the juices run clear. Let the chicken cool. Cover and refrigerate until ready to grill. Refrigerate the remaining barbecue sauce. (The chicken can be prepared to this point up to 1 day ahead.)

Preheat the grill to medium and brush with oil.

Grill the chicken, skin side down, for 5 minutes. Turn the chicken over and brush with barbecue sauce. Continue grilling and basting, for 12 to 15 minutes, or until the skin is crisp. Transfer to a platter and serve.

NEW MEXICO BARBECUE SAUCE

3 tablespoons olive oil

1 cup finely chopped onions

3 garlic cloves, minced

⅔ cup beer

⅓ cup cider vinegar

2 imported bay leaves

1¾ cups ketchup

⅓ cup mild or medium-hot pure red chile powder

2 tablespoons packed brown sugar

2 tablespoons tamari or soy sauce

2 teaspoons ground cumin

1 teaspoon ground coriander

½ teaspoon ground allspice

½ teaspoon ground cloves

One 3- to 3½-pound chicken, quartered

Serves 4

CHICKEN

PREPARE THE RED CHILE SAUCE: In a large skillet, pan-roast the chiles over medium-low heat, turning often, for about 2 minutes, or until browned, making sure the chiles do not blacken; remove. When cool, remove the stems and seeds, and put into a small bowl. Pour the boiling water over, cover, and set aside for 20 minutes, or until soft.

In a food processor or blender, process the chiles with their liquid until smooth. Press the puree through a strainer into a small bowl and set aside.

In a large skillet, heat the oil over medium heat. Add the onions and garlic and cook, stirring, for 2 minutes, or until softened. Add the flour and cook, whisking, for about 1 minute, or until a thick light brown roux forms. Whisk in the beer, stirring. When the mixture boils, add the oregano, salt, and the reserved chile puree. Reduce the heat and simmer for 8 minutes, stirring, until a smooth, thick sauce forms. Transfer to a medium-size bowl and cool.

In a baking dish, combine the chicken and 1 cup of the red chile sauce, stirring until evenly coated. Cover with plastic wrap and marinate in the refrigerator for at least 2 or up to 24 hours. Cover and refrigerate the remaining red chile sauce.

Preheat the grill to medium and brush with oil. Thread the chicken onto the skewers and grill, turning several times, for 5 minutes, until cooked through. Reheat the red chile sauce in a saucepan. Put the skewers on a platter, pour the red chile sauce into a bowl, and serve.

There is a long ristra of New Mexico dried chiles that hangs from my neighbor's back porch. Throughout the fall and winter, he snips chiles from the bottom of the ristra and uses them to make traditional red chile sauce or to flavor stews and soups. This is my version of red sauce, using those very same chiles. Although red chile sauce can be made with chile powder, I much prefer the pungent earthy flavor of whole dried chiles.

RED CHILE SAUCE
6 dried red New Mexico chiles
1 cup boiling water
1 tablespoon olive oil
½ cup chopped onions
3 garlic cloves, minced
1 tablespoon all-purpose flour

1 cup beer or cold water
½ teaspoon dried oregano
½ teaspoon salt

4 boneless skinless chicken breast halves (about 1¼ pounds), cut into 1-inch chunks

Serves 4

O N A WORK SURFACE, put the chicken between 2 pieces of plastic wrap and lightly pound to a uniform thickness. Put into a shallow baking dish.

Prepare the three-citrus habanero marinade: In a small bowl, combine all the marinade ingredients, whisking until blended. Pour over the chicken, turning to coat on both sides. Cover and marinate in the refrigerator for at least 2 or up to 6 hours.

Preheat the grill to medium and brush with oil.

Grill the chicken for 4 to 5 minutes on each side, or until nicely marked and cooked through. Remove to a warm platter and garnish with the cilantro sprigs. Serve accompanied by peach salsa, if using.

The habanero chile is said to be the hottest chile in the world. Here it is used to flavor and add heat to a tangy marinade. The result is succulent citrus-grilled chicken with just an edge of heat.

4 boneless skinless chicken breast halves (5 to 6 ounces each)

THREE CITRUS HABANERO MARINADE
1 teaspoon grated lemon zest
1 teaspoon grated lime zest
1 teaspoon grated orange zest
⅓ cup fresh lemon juice
⅓ cup fresh orange juice

¼ cup fresh lime juice
2 tablespoons olive oil
2 teaspoons honey
1 habanero chile, seeded & coarsely chopped*
⅛ teaspoon freshly ground pepper

4 sprigs fresh cilantro, for garnish
Peach Salsa (page 103), optional

*Fresh habanero chiles range in color from dark green to orange to deep red. Because of their extreme heat, be sure to wear rubber gloves when handling them.

CHICKEN BURRITOS

This has become a favorite chicken " sandwich". The relish lends an old-fashioned sweet and vinegary flavor and the serrano chile and fresh ginger add plenty of bite.

Serves 4

PREPARE THE SWEET PEPPER RELISH: In a medium-size nonreactive saucepan, bring the vinegar, sugar, ginger, garlic, chile, cumin, salt, and bay leaf to a boil over medium-high heat. Add the bell peppers and onion, stirring to combine. Reduce the heat to low and simmer, uncovered, for 2 minutes. Discard the bay leaf, transfer the relish to a bowl, and cool to room temperature.

Place the chicken between 2 pieces of plastic wrap and pound to a uniform thickness. Put into a shallow nonreactive baking dish and pour the marinade over, turning to coat. Cover and marinate in the refrigerator for at least 2 or up to 24 hours.

Preheat the grill to medium and brush with oil.

Grill the chicken for 4 to 5 minutes on each side, or until cooked through. Transfer to a dish and cover.

Grill the tortillas for about 10 seconds on each side, or until puffed. Cover to keep warm.

Shred the chicken, place along the center of the tortillas, and top with pepper relish, avocado, and cilantro. Roll up and serve.

SWEET PEPPER RELISH

½ cup cider vinegar

1 tablespoon sugar

1 tablespoon coarsely chopped peeled fresh ginger

3 garlic cloves, coarsely chopped

1 serrano chile, seeded & chopped

½ teaspoon cumin seeds

½ teaspoon salt

1 bay leaf

1 each red & green bell pepper, cored, seeded & chopped

1 cup coarsely chopped red onion

4 boneless skinless chicken breast halves (about 6 ounces each)

1 recipe Three Citrus Habanero Marinade (page 33)

4 flour tortillas (8 to 10 inches in diameter)

2 small avocados, halved, pitted, peeled & cut crosswise into ¼-inch-wide slices

Cilantro leaves, for garnish (optional)

Serves 6

P REPARE THE PUMPKIN SEED PESTO: In a food processor or blender, combine the pumpkin seeds, cilantro, onion, garlic, cumin seeds, and salt. Pulse until the mixture is finely ground. With the machine running, add the olive oil in a steady stream, processing until a paste forms. Transfer the pesto to a small bowl.

Place the turkey breast skin side up on a work surface. Using your fingers, gently separate the skin from the turkey meat. Spread 1 cup of the pumpkin seed pesto evenly over the meat. Turn the turkey breast over and spread the remaining pumpkin seed pesto over it. Beginning with a long side, roll the turkey up, jelly-roll style. Using kitchen string, tie the turkey roll at 2-inch intervals.

Preheat the grill to medium-low and set up the rotisserie attachment. Place a drip pan slightly larger than the turkey roll on the grill grate.

Put the turkey on the spit and grill for 1 hour and 45 minutes, or until a meat thermometer registers 160°F, basting the turkey several times with the drippings that accumulate in the pan. Remove the turkey from the spit, cover, and let rest on a cutting board for 10 minutes.

Using a sharp knife, cut the turkey into ½-inch-thick slices. Transfer to a platter and serve hot.

Pumpkin seeds have been used in Mexican cooking since Mayan times and are a traditional ingredient in moles and sauces. Here, their uniquely nutty flavor blends well with garlic and cilantro to make a paste that is spread over a boned turkey breast, as well as under the skin. The turkey breast is then rolled, tied, and grilled rotisserie-style.

PUMPKIN SEED PESTO
1 cup roasted pumpkin seeds
1 cup loosely packed fresh cilantro leaves
½ medium-size onion, coarsely chopped

3 garlic cloves
½ teaspoon cumin seeds
½ teaspoon salt
⅓ cup olive oil

One 5-pound boneless turkey breast

NOTE: The turkey breast can also be grilled over indirect heat (page 18) in a foil pan.

GREEN CHILE SAUCE

TURKEY WITH

New Mexican restaurants serve green chile sauce on top of everything from cheese enchiladas to fried eggs to pork stew. One of my favorite ways to eat it is with thin slices of grilled pounded turkey breast. The sauce can be made ahead and it also freezes well.

Serves 4

PREHEAT THE GRILL to medium and brush with oil.

Prepare the green chile sauce: In a large skillet, heat the oil over medium heat. Cook the onions and garlic, stirring, for 2 to 3 minutes, or until soft and translucent. Add the flour and whisk constantly until smooth, bubbling, and light brown. Whisk in the water and green chiles. When the sauce begins to simmer, reduce the heat to low and stir in the cumin and salt. Cook, stirring often, for 3 to 4 minutes, or until the sauce thickens. Transfer to a food processor and pulse several times, or until the sauce is almost smooth. Transfer to a small saucepan and keep warm over very low heat.

On a work surface, cut the turkey across the grain into ¼-inch-thick strips. Place the turkey strips between 2 pieces of plastic wrap and lightly pound to ⅛-inch thickness. Season with salt and pepper.

Grill the turkey slices for about 1 minute on each side, or until just cooked through. Remove to a small platter, pour the green chile sauce over, and serve.

GREEN CHILE SAUCE
2 tablespoons vegetable oil
⅔ cup chopped onions
3 garlic cloves, minced
1 tablespoon all-purpose flour
1 cup cold water
8 mild, medium, or hot New Mexico green chiles, grilled, peeled, cored, seeded & chopped (page 24)

¼ teaspoon ground cumin
½ teaspoon salt

1 to 1¼ pounds turkey tenders*
Salt & pepper

NOTE: Green chile sauce will keep, tightly covered in the refrigerator, for 3 to 5 days. Or freeze for up to 1 month.

*Packaged turkey tenders are available in most supermarkets.

Serves 4

Duck is often served with an overly sweet sauce that completely masks its delicate flavor. This red chile–plum sauce is neither too sweet nor too spicy, and therefore the perfect counterpoint to the smoky grilled meat.

PLACE THE DUCK BETWEEN pieces of plastic wrap and pound to an even thickness. Score the skin of each breast, making parallel cuts 1 inch apart.

Prepare the red wine marinade: Combine all the marinade ingredients in a baking dish and add the duck. Cover and marinate in the refrigerator for at least 1 or up to 8 hours.

Prepare the chile-plum sauce: In a small skillet, pan-roast the chiles over medium-low heat, turning, for 2 minutes, or until puffed. When cool, remove the stems and seeds.

Preheat the grill to medium-high and brush with oil.

In a medium-size saucepan, combine the plums, apple juice, garlic, chile powder, brown sugar, and salt. Add the chiles and bring to a boil over medium-high heat. Reduce the heat and simmer, uncovered, for 15 minutes, or until the plums are tender. Transfer the mixture to a food processor and process until smooth. Press through a strainer into a serving bowl and keep warm.

Grill the duck for about 2 minutes on each side, or until seared. Grill 5 minutes longer on each side, or until medium-rare. Transfer to a cutting board, cover, and let rest for 5 minutes. Thinly slice the duck. Spoon some plum sauce onto each serving plate, arrange the duck, and serve.

4 boneless duck breasts (6 ounces each), excess fat trimmed

RED WINE MARINADE

1½ cups dry red wine

3 garlic cloves, thinly sliced

3 whole allspice berries, crushed

½ teaspoon whole black peppercorns, crushed

½ teaspoon dried oregano

CHILE-PLUM SAUCE

3 dried cascabel chiles

3 firm but ripe red plums, halved, pitted & cut into 1-inch chunks

1½ cups unsweetened apple juice

1 garlic clove, chopped

1 tablespoon mild pure chile powder

2 teaspoons packed brown sugar

½ teaspoon salt

STEAK SALAD

Steak salad has long been a favorite of mine and it is a lighter way to enjoy a good piece of grilled beef. The addition of cumin, chile powder, and pinto beans makes this a classic Southwestern salad.

Serves 4

PUT THE STEAK INTO a shallow baking dish.

Prepare the marinade: In a small bowl, whisk together all the marinade ingredients. Pour over the steak, cover, and marinate in the refrigerator for at least 2 or up to 24 hours, turning occasionally.

In a small skillet, toast the pine nuts, stirring often, over medium-low heat, for about 2 minutes, or until golden. Transfer to a small dish and set aside.

Preheat the grill to high and brush with oil. Bring a medium-size saucepan of salted water to a boil over high heat. Add the green beans and carrots and cook for 5 minutes, or until just tender. Drain and plunge into a bowl of cold water. When cool, drain and put into a large bowl. Add the watercress, mushrooms, bell peppers, and pinto beans, tossing. Set aside.

Grill the steak for 2 to 3 minutes on each side for medium-rare, or 3 to 4 minutes on each side for medium. Meanwhile, grill the onion, turning several times, for about 5 minutes, or until lightly blistered, browned, and beginning to soften. Remove the steak

1 pound New York strip steak

MARINADE
½ cup dry red wine
3 garlic cloves, minced
1 tablespoon coarsely ground medium-hot pure chiles
1 teaspoon chopped fresh oregano
½ teaspoon ground cumin
¼ teaspoon salt
⅛ teaspoon freshly ground pepper

3 tablespoons pine nuts
½ pound green beans, trimmed
2 carrots, halved lengthwise & cut diagonally into ⅛-inch-thick slices
2 bunches watercress, trimmed & washed
8 medium-size button mushrooms, trimmed & thinly sliced
½ each red & yellow bell pepper, halved, cored, seeded & julienned
1 cup cooked pinto beans, drained & rinsed if canned
1 small red onion, halved
¼ cup crumbled blue cheese

to a platter, cover, and let rest for about 5 minutes. Remove the onion to a cutting board, and when cool enough to handle, coarsely chop. Add to the vegetable mixture.

Cut the steak across the grain into long thin slices. Set aside. Briefly whisk the dressing and drizzle over the vegetables, tossing until well mixed. Divide the vegetables among serving plates and arrange the sliced steak on top. Sprinkle with the blue cheese and pine nuts, and serve.

RED WINE DRESSING

PREPARE THE RED WINE DRESSING: In a small bowl, whisk the vinegar, mustard, and garlic. Add the oil slowly, whisking until creamy. Add the rosemary and pepper; set aside.

This flavorful dressing will enliven grilled chicken, salmon, veal, or a bitter greens salad.

RED WINE DRESSING

3 tablespoons red wine vinegar

1 tablespoon Dijon mustard

1 garlic clove, minced

⅓ cup extra-virgin olive oil

2 teaspoons chopped fresh rosemary

⅛ teaspoon freshly ground pepper

Serves 4

It is difficult to improve upon grilled tenderloin of beef, but this red chile rub succeeds admirably. The rub ingredients blend to form a subtle dark smokiness just discernible under the rich beef flavor.

PUT THE FILLET STEAKS into a shallow baking dish.

Prepare the red chile rub: In a spice grinder or mortar and pestle, combine all the rub ingredients and process or pound until finely ground. Spread the rub evenly over both sides of the beef. Cover and refrigerate for at least 2 or up to 6 hours.

Preheat the grill to medium-high, set a vegetable grill rack on top, and brush with oil.

Prepare the avocado salsa: Grill the tomatoes and jalapeños, turning occasionally, for 4 to 7 minutes, or until the skins are browned. Remove and set aside until cool enough to handle.

Cut the tomatoes into ½-inch dice and put into a medium-size bowl. Mince the jalapeños and add to the bowl. Add the avocados, cilantro, garlic, and salt, mixing gently. Cover with plastic wrap and set aside.

Grill the fillet steaks for 4 minutes on each side for rare (110°F on a meat thermometer), or to the desired degree of doneness. Remove to a plate.

To serve, place some arugula leaves in the center of each serving plate. Put a fillet steak on top and spoon some avocado salsa on the top. Serve hot.

Four 1-inch thick beef fillet steaks (about 6 ounces each)

RED CHILE RUB

⅓ cup mild or medium-hot pure chile powder

1 tablespoon dried oregano

2 garlic cloves, minced

2 teaspoons sugar

¾ teaspoon kosher salt

AVOCADO SALSA

2 plum tomatoes, halved

2 jalapeño chiles, halved, seeded & ribs removed

2 medium-size ripe avocados, halved, pitted, peeled & cut into ½-inch cubes

2 tablespoons chopped fresh cilantro

1 garlic clove, minced

⅛ teaspoon salt

1 large bunch arugula, trimmed, washed & dried

BEEF FAJITAS

Fajitas are finger food. To thoroughly enjoy this dish, put the grilled steak on warm tortillas, sprinkle with scallions and fresh cilantro, top with a dollop of sour cream, and roll up. To add a little heat, serve bowls of pico de gallo and chopped grilled jalapeño chiles alongside.

Serves 4

PUT THE SKIRT STEAK in a shallow baking dish.

In a small bowl, combine the lime juice, scallions, jalapeños, and salt. Pour over the steak, turning to coat evenly. Cover and marinate in the refrigerator for at least 30 minutes or up to 1 hour.

Preheat the grill to high and brush with oil.

Grill the steak for 2 minutes on each side for medium-rare or to desired doneness. Remove to a cutting board, cover, and let rest for about 5 minutes.

Meanwhile, grill the tortillas for about 10 seconds on each side, or until lightly charred and puffy. Transfer to a plate and cover to keep warm.

Cut the steak across the grain into thin slices and transfer to a platter. Serve immediately accompanied by the tortillas, sour cream, cilantro, scallions, pico de gallo, and grilled jalapeños, if desired.

1 pound skirt steak

⅓ cup fresh lime juice

¼ cup chopped scallions

2 jalapeño chiles, seeded & chopped

¼ teaspoon salt

8 small flour tortillas

¾ cup low-fat sour cream

Chopped fresh cilantro & chopped scallions, for garnish

Pico de Gallo (page 96), optional

Grilled jalapeño chiles

PORK TENDERLOIN

Serves 4

PUT THE PORK INTO a shallow baking dish. Pour 1 cup of the chile sauce over, turning to coat well on all sides. Cover with plastic wrap and marinate in the refrigerator for at least 4 or up to 24 hours, turning occasionally. Cover and refrigerate the remaining chile sauce.

Preheat the grill to medium and brush with oil.

Grill the pork, turning several times, for 25 to 35 minutes, or until cooked through but still moist. A meat thermometer inserted into the center of the meat should register 160°F.

Meanwhile, heat the reserved chile sauce in a small saucepan over low heat until hot.

Put the pork on a cutting board, cover loosely with foil, and let rest for about 5 minutes.

Cut the pork into thin slices and transfer to a small platter. Transfer the red chile sauce to a serving bowl and pass separately.

Traditionally, carne adovada is a pork stew made with pork chops or pork shoulder that is marinated and then baked in a red chile sauce. In this more elegant version, pork tenderloin is marinated in red chile sauce and then grilled. Serve the spicy succulent pork thinly sliced and accompanied by Lemon–Oregano Potatoes (page 81) or Southwestern Tabbouleh (page 84).

**One 1½-pound pork
tenderloin**

**1 recipe Red Chile Sauce
(page 31)**

ONION SALSA

Serves 4 to 6

I used to think that grilling pork chops would make them dry, but this recipe deliciously proves the opposite. Grilling has now become my favorite way to cook pork chops. The apple cider marinade also keeps them moist.

PUT THE PORK CHOPS into a shallow baking dish.

Prepare the apple cider marinade: In a medium-size bowl, whisk together all the marinade ingredients. Pour over the pork chops, cover with plastic wrap, and marinate in the refrigerator for at least 4 or up to 24 hours, turning the chops occasionally.

Preheat the grill to medium-hot. Place a vegetable grill rack on top and brush with oil.

Prepare the red onion salsa: Brush the onion slices and garlic cloves with the oil. Grill the onion and garlic for about 6 minutes, or until lightly browned and softened. Remove from the grill and set aside until cool.

Coarsely chop the onions and garlic and put into a medium-size bowl. Add the remaining salsa ingredients and mix well. Set aside.

Grill the chops for 5 to 7 minutes on each side, or until just cooked through. Remove to a platter and serve accompanied by the salsa.

Six ¾-inch thick center cut pork chops

APPLE CIDER MARINADE

1½ cups apple cider

½ cup dry sherry

2 tablespoons mild pure chile powder

2 tablespoons olive oil

6 whole black peppercorns

2 imported bay leaves

½ teaspoon salt

GRILLED RED ONION SALSA

1 pound small red onions, cut into ¼-inch-thick slices

6 garlic cloves

2 tablespoons olive oil

¼ cup apple cider

¼ cup dry sherry

2 tablespoons red wine vinegar

2 tablespoons sherry vinegar

2 tablespoons chopped fresh cilantro

2 tablespoons chopped fresh parsley

¼ teaspoon salt

¼ teaspoon freshly ground pepper

PEPPER RUBBED TUNA

Serves 4

PREPARE THE BLACK PEPPER and cumin rub: Put the cumin, peppercorns, and oregano in a small skillet and toast over medium heat, stirring, for about 2 minutes, or until fragrant. Transfer to a spice grinder or mortar and pestle and pulse or pound until the spices are ground medium-fine. Transfer to a small bowl and add the tamari and honey, blending until a paste forms.

Put the tuna steaks on a plate and coat with the rub, spreading it evenly over both sides. Cover with plastic wrap and marinate in the refrigerator for at least 30 minutes or up to 2 hours.

Meanwhile, preheat the grill to medium and brush with oil.

Grill the tuna for 3 to 4 minutes on each side for medium, until barely pink in the center, or to the desired degree of doneness. Serve immediately.

Soy and honey, along with the crushed black peppercorns and cumin seeds, are blended together to form a delicious coating for these tuna steaks. No one seasoning dominates here; rather they combine to create a more complex flavor.

BLACK PEPPER AND CUMIN RUB

¼ cup cumin seeds

3 tablespoons whole black peppercorns

1 teaspoon dried oregano

¼ cup tamari or soy sauce

2 tablespoons honey

Four 1-inch-thick tuna steaks (6 to 8 ounces each)

ROASTED TOMATOES

SWORDFISH &

Preparing an herb butter with roasted tomato and fresh rosemary is an easy and flavorful way to dress up simply grilled swordfish. The butter would also be delicious on grilled chicken or lamb.

PUT THE SWORDFISH into a shallow baking dish.

Prepare the marinade: In a small bowl, combine the tamari, oil, garlic, and cumin, whisking until blended. Pour over the swordfish, turning to coat evenly. Cover with plastic wrap and marinate in the refrigerator for at least 2 or up to 8 hours.

Preheat the grill to medium-high and brush with oil.

Prepare the roasted tomato butter: Grill the tomato, turning several times, for about 10 minutes, or until the skin is charred and the tomato is beginning to soften. Remove from the grill and set aside. When cool, chop the tomato and put into a small bowl along with the butter, rosemary, and pepper. Use a fork or the back of a wooden spoon to mix the ingredients until well blended. (The butter will turn pinkish-orange, with specks of tomato throughout.) Use a rubber spatula to scrape the butter onto a small square of plastic wrap. Shape the butter into a cylinder about 1 inch in diameter, twist the ends of the plastic wrap tightly to enclose the butter, and refrigerate for at least 1 hour, or freeze for 30 minutes, until firm.

Grill the swordfish for 3 to 4 minutes on each side, brushing with the marinade during the first 4 minutes, until just slightly pink in the center, or to the desired degree of doneness. Remove the swordfish to serving plates and top each with a thick slice of the tomato butter.

Four ¾-inch-thick swordfish steaks (about 6 ounces each)

MARINADE

3 tablespoons tamari or soy sauce

1 tablespoon olive oil

2 garlic cloves, chopped

½ teaspoon ground cumin

ROASTED TOMATO BUTTER

1 plum tomato

6 tablespoons unsalted butter, at room temperature

2 teaspoons chopped fresh rosemary

¼ teaspoon freshly ground pepper

CHIPOTLE RUBBED

Serves 4

PREHEAT THE GRILL to medium and brush with oil.

Prepare the chipotle-vinegar rub: In a small skillet, pan-roast the chipotle chiles over medium heat, turning them often, for 1 to 2 minutes, or until puffed and fragrant. Remove the chiles from the pan and set aside. When the chiles are cool enough to handle, remove the stems and seeds. Transfer the chiles to a spice grinder or mortar and pestle and process or pound until ground. In a small bowl, combine the ground chiles, sugar, salt, cumin, and pepper. Add the vinegar and whisk until blended.

Put the snapper fillets into a shallow baking dish. Brush the chipotle-vinegar rub on both sides of the fillets.

Grill the snapper fillets for 2 to 3 minutes on each side, or until opaque throughout and lightly charred in spots. Transfer to a platter and serve hot.

There are more than a hundred species of snapper, but there is only one true red snapper. It is found in the warm waters of the Atlantic and in the Gulf of Mexico. Many similar species are sold under the same name. Fortunately, most of these cousins also have a delicious taste and a firm meaty texture that is perfect for grilling and stands up well to the vibrant flavors in this rub.

CHIPOTLE-VINEGAR RUB

3 dried chipotle chiles

1 teaspoon coarsely ground mild pure chiles

1 teaspoon sugar

1 teaspoon salt

½ teaspoon ground cumin

¼ teaspoon freshly ground pepper

¼ cup cider vinegar

4 red snapper fillets (about 6 ounces each)

SHRIMP TACOS

Serves 4

TEQUILA

Tequila and citrus are natural partners. Here, it's fresh orange juice that mellows tequila's punch to prevent the marinade from overwhelming the delicate flavor of the shrimp.

PREPARE THE TEQUILA MARINADE: In a medium-size bowl, combine all the marinade ingredients and whisk until combined. Add the shrimp, tossing until well coated. Cover with plastic wrap and marinate in the refrigerator for at least 2 or up to 24 hours.

Preheat the grill to high and brush with oil. Soak four 10-inch bamboo skewers in cold water for at least 30 minutes.

Thread the shrimp, cherry tomatoes, and chiles alternately onto the skewers. Grill for 3 to 4 minutes on each side, brushing once or twice with the marinade, or until the shrimp are bright pink and firm to touch and the peppers are lightly browned and slightly softened. Remove and keep warm. Grill the tortillas for about 20 seconds on each side, or until puffed.

To serve, remove the shrimp, tomatoes, and chiles from the skewers and put onto the warm tortillas. Squeeze some lime juice over and roll the tortillas up for eating.

TEQUILA MARINADE

- ⅓ cup tequila
- 3 tablespoons fresh orange juice
- 2 tablespoons rice wine vinegar
- 1 tablespoon olive oil
- 2 teaspoons grated orange zest
- 1 teaspoon coarsely ground hot pure chiles
- ⅛ teaspoon salt

- ¾ pound jumbo shrimp, peeled & deveined
- 12 cherry tomatoes
- 2 Anaheim chiles, cut into 1½-inch lengths
- 8 small flour tortillas
- Lime wedges, for serving

Serves 4

PREHEAT THE GRILL to medium and generously brush with oil.

Prepare the herb crust: In a food processor, combine all the herb crust ingredients, pulsing 2 or 3 times, or until a coarse paste forms.

Place the salmon skin side down on a tray. Using your hands, spread the herb paste over the top of the salmon fillet, making a thick, even layer.

Transfer the salmon to the grill, crust side down, and grill for 3 minutes. Use 2 metal spatulas to gently loosen the salmon from the grill and turn it over. Grill the salmon for 3 to 4 minutes longer, or just until opaque throughout. Use the spatulas to carefully remove the fish from the grill to a warm platter. Garnish with the lemon and lime wedges and serve.

Bright red-fleshed coho salmon has a slightly stronger flavor than other varieties of salmon. It matches perfectly with the robust flavor of the sun-dried tomatoes, garlic, and chiles in the herb crust. If you have a fish grilling basket, this would be the perfect time to use it. Be sure to oil basket generously to prevent the salmon from sticking.

HERB CRUST

- 1 cup chopped oil-packed sun-dried tomatoes
- ½ cup loosely packed fresh basil leaves
- ½ cup loosely packed fresh parsley leaves
- 3 tablespoons fresh oregano leaves
- 3 garlic cloves
- 2 tablespoons coarsely ground medium-hot pure chiles

- 2 pounds coho or other salmon fillet (about ¾ inch thick), in one piece, with skin
- Lemon & lime wedges, for garnish

MARINATED SALMON

I love to grill salmon steaks generously coated with chopped fresh herbs. The combination of dill, basil, and cilantro in this recipe forms a flavorful topping that keeps the salmon moist and juicy.

PUT THE SALMON STEAKS into a shallow baking dish.

Prepare the fresh herb marinade: In a small bowl, whisk together the wine, oil, coarsely ground chiles, salt, and pepper. Add the dill, basil, and cilantro, stirring until well mixed. Pour the marinade over the salmon, turning to coat on all sides. Cover with plastic wrap and marinate in the refrigerator for at least 2 or up to 24 hours, turning occasionally.

Preheat the grill to medium and brush generously with oil.

Grill the salmon for 3 to 4 minutes on each side, or until firm to the touch and just barely cooked in the center. Transfer to a platter and serve immediately.

Four 1-inch-thick
  salmon steaks (about
  6 ounces each)

FRESH HERB MARINADE

1 cup dry white wine

1 tablespoon olive oil

1 tablespoon coarsely ground
  medium-hot pure chiles

¼ teaspoon salt

¼ teaspoon freshly ground
  pepper

½ cup coarsely chopped
  fresh dill

½ cup coarsely chopped
  fresh basil

½ cup coarsely chopped
  fresh cilantro

CHILE-LIME BUTTER

Serves 4

BRING A LARGE POT OF WATER to a rolling boil over high heat. Plunge the lobsters head first into the water and cook for 3 to 4 minutes, or until bright red. Remove the lobsters and plunge into a large bowl of cold water to stop the cooking. Drain in a colander, put into a large bowl and cover. Refrigerate.

Prepare the chile lime butter: Melt the butter in a small saucepan over medium heat. Remove from the heat and stir in the cilantro, lime juice, and chile powder. Set aside.

Preheat the grill to high and brush with oil.

Place a lobster on its back on a cutting board. Using a large sharp knife, split the lobster down the middle, being careful not to cut completely through the shell. Remove the black vein and the sand sac located near the head. Repeat with the remaining lobsters. Baste the lobster meat with some of the chile butter.

Grill the lobsters, flesh side down, for 6 to 8 minutes, or until the flesh is just beginning to look opaque. Turn the lobsters over, baste with more chile butter, and continue to cook for 1 to 2 minutes longer, or until the lobsters are cooked through. Transfer the lobster to a large warm platter and garnish with lime wedges and cilantro sprigs. Transfer the remaining chile butter to a small serving dish and pass separately.

Whole grilled lobsters don't need too many extras to become a fantastic meal. Serve with Cumin–Orange Bean Salad (page 80), some warm fresh tortillas, and lots of the Chile Lime Butter.

Four 1-pound live lobsters

CHILE LIME BUTTER
½ cup (1 stick) unsalted butter
¼ cup chopped fresh cilantro

2 tablespoons fresh lime juice
2 teaspoons medium-hot pure chile powder

Lime wedges & cilantro sprigs, for garnish

SCALLOP SALAD

Nutty Texmati rice tossed with grilled peppers, snap peas, chiles, and jícama and topped with grilled sea scallops makes a spectacular dish. A lightly seasoned tomatillo salsa served alongside adds a refreshing accent.

Serves 4

PREPARE THE ORANGE and balsamic marinade: Whisk all the marinade ingredients in a medium-size bowl. Add the scallops and toss to coat. Cover and marinate in the refrigerator for 1 hour.

Bring a medium-size saucepan of water to a boil. Add the snap peas and cook for about 30 seconds, or until bright green. Drain the snap peas, then plunge into a bowl of cold water to stop the cooking .When cool, drain and set aside.

Preheat the grill to medium-high and brush with oil. Soak four 8-inch bamboo skewers in cold water for at least 30 minutes.

Grill the bell peppers and the chile, skin side down, for 3 to 4 minutes, or until nicely browned. Remove, and when cool, cut into ½-inch-wide strips. Transfer to a large bowl and add the snap peas, scallions, jícama, parsley, and rice, tossing until mixed. Drizzle with the oil and vinegar, season with salt and pepper, and toss. Set aside.

Thread the scallops onto the skewers and grill for 3 to 5 minutes, or until opaque throughout. Divide the rice salad among serving plates. Top each with a skewer of scallops and pass the salsa alongside.

ORANGE AND BALSAMIC MARINADE
¼ cup fresh orange juice
1 tablespoon balsamic vinegar
2 teaspoons olive oil
1 garlic clove, thinly sliced

¾ pound sea scallops

3 ounces snap peas or snow peas, strings removed
½ each red & yellow bell pepper, cored & seeded
1 Anaheim chile, cored, seeded & ribs removed

3 small scallions, finely chopped
1 small jícama, peeled & cut into 2-x-¼-inch sticks
½ cup finely chopped fresh parsley
2 cups Texmati rice, cooked according to the package directions, rinsed & kept warm
3 tablespoons olive oil
2 tablespoons rice wine vinegar
Salt & freshly ground pepper
Tomatillo Salsa (page 28)

WITH SAGE

TROUT

I love the subtle and uncomplicated flavor of trout, especially when it is grilled. Here, brushed with a white wine, mustard, and sage marinade and served with lemon, it becomes a simple and delicious main course.

Serves 4

ARRANGE THE TROUT, flat open and skin side down, in a large shallow baking dish.

Prepare the white wine marinade: In a small bowl, whisk together the wine, mustard, coarsely ground chiles, and pepper. Stir in the sage. Pour the mixture evenly over the trout, turning to coat evenly. Cover with plastic wrap and marinate in the refrigerator for at least 30 minutes or up to 2 hours.

Preheat the grill to medium and brush with oil.

Place the trout flat open on the grill, skin side down, and grill, without turning the fish, for 3 to 5 minutes, or until the flesh is firm and no longer translucent. Transfer the trout to serving plates, and garnish with lemon wedges and sage leaves.

4 boneless whole trout (about 8 ounces each), heads & tails removed

WHITE WINE MARINADE

⅓ cup dry white wine

1 tablespoon Dijon mustard

¼ teaspoon coarsely ground pure chiles

¼ teaspoon freshly ground pepper

10 to 12 fresh sage leaves, julienned

Lemon wedges & additional fresh sage leaves, for garnish

VEGETABLES & SALADS

Serves 4

This is a salad to be made at the height of corn season, which in New Mexico is mercilessly short. It is not until late August that the farmers' pickup trucks first arrive at the outdoor markets heaped with corn, but it is always worth the wait.

PREHEAT THE GRILL to medium and brush with oil.

Bring a large pot of water to a boil over high heat. Cook the corn for 3 minutes. Drain.

Grill the corn, turning several times, for 5 to 6 minutes, or until it has begun to darken on all sides. Remove and set aside until cool enough to handle.

Using a sharp knife, cut off the corn kernels and put into a medium-size bowl. Add the tomatoes, sun-dried tomatoes, scallion, cilantro, parsley, salt, and pepper, then add the lime juice, stirring until well mixed. Transfer the corn salad to a serving bowl and sprinkle with the sprouts, if using. This salad is delicious served either warm or at room temperature, but it is best served the day it is made.

4 ears fresh corn, husks & silk removed

2 plum tomatoes, halved lengthwise & cut crosswise into ¼-inch-thick slices

⅓ cup julienned oil-packed sun-dried tomatoes

1 scallion, chopped

2 tablespoons chopped fresh cilantro

2 tablespoons chopped fresh parsley

¼ teaspoon salt

¼ teaspoon freshly ground pepper

3 tablespoons fresh lime juice

Sunflower or other sprouts, for garnish (optional)

CORN & LENTIL SALAD

Serves 6

This lentil salad tastes best freshly made, but can be held in the refrigerator for up to twenty four hours. It makes a great side dish to serve alongside Trout with Sage (page 60), or Pepper Rubbed Tuna (page 49).

PREHEAT THE GRILL to medium and brush with oil.

In a medium-size saucepan, combine the lentils with water to cover by ½ inch and bring to a boil over medium heat. Cook, uncovered, for 12 to 15 minutes, or until tender. Drain the lentils in a colander, rinse under cold water, drain again, and set aside.

Brush the corn with 2 teaspoons of the oil and sprinkle with the chile rub, coating the corn evenly. Grill the corn and bell pepper, turning often, for 4 to 6 minutes, or until the corn is browned in spots and the bell pepper is blistered and brown. Set aside to cool.

Using a sharp knife, cut the corn kernels from the cobs. Peel, core, seed, and chop the bell pepper. In a large bowl, combine the lentils and chickpeas. Add the corn and bell pepper.

In a small bowl, whisk together the lemon juice, garlic, tarragon, oregano, salt, and pepper. Add the remaining 3 tablespoons oil, whisking until well blended. Pour the vinaigrette over the lentil salad, tossing well. The salad can be served at room temperature or chilled.

1 cup lentils

2 ears fresh corn, husks & silk removed

3 tablespoons plus 2 teaspoons olive oil

2 teaspoons Red Chile Rub (page 106)

1 small red bell pepper

1 cup cooked chickpeas, drained & rinsed if canned

3 tablespoons fresh lemon juice

1 garlic clove, minced

2 tablespoons chopped fresh tarragon

2 teaspoons chopped fresh oregano

¼ teaspoon salt

¼ teaspoon freshly ground pepper

Serves 6

Our friends from Mexico often serve shredded green cabbage, chopped onion, and sliced radishes mixed together as a garnish for soup. Here, the same ingredients are tossed together with sherry vinegar, olive oil, chopped jalapeño chiles, and apple slices to make an outstanding cabbage slaw— the perfect accompaniment to grilled snapper or trout.

PREHEAT THE GRILL to medium and brush with oil.

Grill the bell peppers, poblano chile, and onion, turning often, for 5 to 7 minutes, or until the poblano is blistered and brown, and the bell peppers and onion are grill-marked and softened. Wrap the poblano chile in a paper towel, seal tightly in a plastic bag, and let steam for 10 minutes. Remove the chile and let cool.

Meanwhile, in a large bowl, combine the savoy and red cabbages, apple, radishes, jalapeño chiles, and parsley.

When the bell peppers are cool enough to handle, halve, core and cut into ¼-inch-wide strips. Remove the stem and seeds from the poblano chile and chop. Cut the onion into ½-inch dice. Add the bell peppers, poblano chile, and onion to the cabbage.

In a small bowl, whisk together the oil and vinegar. Pour over the vegetables, tossing until well combined. Season with salt and pepper, toss again, and serve. (The slaw can be covered and refrigerated for up to 8 hours. Toss just before serving and season again with salt and pepper if needed.)

1 red bell pepper, halved, cored & seeded	1 small apple, halved, cored & cut crosswise into paper-thin slices
1 green bell pepper, halved, cored & seeded	4 radishes, thinly sliced
1 poblano chile	2 jalapeño chiles, seeded & finely chopped
½ medium-size red onion	¼ cup chopped fresh parsley
4 cups shredded savoy cabbage	¼ cup olive oil
2 cups chopped red cabbage	¼ cup sherry vinegar
	Salt & freshly ground pepper

SALAD

Serves 4

This classic salad is made new again with the addition of grilled shrimp. The dressing, made without the usual egg, has just enough bite from two kinds of chiles to satisfy without overpowering the salad ingredients.

PREPARE THE SHRIMP MARINADE: In a bowl, combine the marinade ingredients. Add the shrimp, tossing. Cover and refrigerate for 1 to 4 hours.

Preheat the oven to 375° F. Preheat the grill to medium-high and brush with oil.

Prepare the croutons: In a medium-size bowl, drizzle the oil over the bread cubes, tossing. Sprinkle with the chile powder and salt and toss. Spread the cubes on a baking sheet. Bake, turning once, for 8 minutes, or until golden. Return to the bowl, sprinkle with the Parmesan, toss, and set aside.

Prepare the Caesar dressing: Toast the cumin seeds in a small skillet for 2 minutes, or until fragrant. Set aside. In a food processor, combine the lime juice, mustard, garlic, anchovies, coarsely ground chiles, cumin, chile powder, and pepper, processing until smooth. With the machine running, add the oil in steady stream, processing until smooth. Transfer to a large bowl and set aside.

Grill the shrimp for 2 minutes on each side, or until firm to the touch. Remove.

Add the lettuce and croutons to the dressing and toss. Divide the salad among serving plates, top with the hard-boiled eggs and shrimp, and serve.

SHRIMP MARINADE
¾ cup beer
1 tablespoon Dijon mustard
2 garlic cloves, minced
2 teaspoons pure chile powder

16 jumbo shrimp, peeled
   & deveined

RED CHILE CROUTONS
2 tablespoons olive oil
4 cups ½-inch bread cubes
1 tablespoon pure chile powder
½ teaspoon salt
2 tablespoons freshly grated
   Parmesan cheese

CAESAR DRESSING
¼ teaspoon cumin seeds
¼ cup fresh lime juice
2 teaspoons Dijon mustard
2 garlic cloves, minced
2 anchovy fillets, mashed
½ teaspoon coarsely ground
   hot pure chiles
¼ teaspoon each medium-hot
   pure chile powder & freshly
   ground pepper
⅓ cup extra-virgin olive oil
10 ounces romaine lettuce,
   torn into 2-inch pieces
2 hard-boiled eggs, quartered

GRILLED LEEKS

If you aren't able to find small tender leeks, purchase larger ones and parboil them for one to two minutes in boiling water. Just be sure to drain them thoroughly before tossing with the vinegar and oil dressing.

Serves 4

PUT THE LEEKS INTO a shallow baking dish. In a small bowl, combine the lime juice, vinegar, and olive oil. Pour the marinade over the leeks and marinate at room temperature for 1 to 1½ hours, turning occasionally.

Preheat the grill to medium and brush with oil.

Place the leeks on the grill, cut side down. Grill, brushing frequently with the marinade, turning once or twice, for 15 to 20 minutes, or until softened and wrinkled. Turn the leeks and grill for 5 to 7 minutes longer, or until very tender. Remove to a serving dish, season with salt and pepper, and serve.

4 leeks (about 1 inch in diameter), white part only, halved lengthwise

3 tablespoons fresh lime juice

2 tablespoons cider vinegar

2 tablespoons olive oil

Salt & freshly ground pepper

Serves 6

The forested mountainous parts of the American Southwest and Mexico produce an array of wild mushrooms. This recipe calls for the more familiar cultivated mushrooms, but use your own favorite mix. If using the smaller, more delicate varieties such as porcinis, adjust the cooking time accordingly.

PREHEAT THE OVEN TO 350°F. Lightly grease a 1½-quart casserole. Preheat the grill to medium, set a vegetable grill rack on top, and brush with oil.

Prepare the fragrant rice: Grill the onion, turning once or twice, for 8 to 10 minutes, or until charred on the outside and almost tender. Meanwhile, grill the tomatoes, turning several times, for 6 to 8 minutes, or until the skins are blistered and blackened. Remove the onion and tomato from the grill. Cool, then cut into ½-inch chunks. Set aside.

In a large skillet, heat the oil over medium heat. Add the rice and cook, stirring, for 2 to 3 minutes, or until the rice is golden Stir in the onion, tomatoes, and the remaining rice ingredients. When the mixture begins to simmer, spoon into the prepared casserole and cover tightly. Bake the rice for 25 minutes, or until the liquid is absorbed and the rice is tender. Remove and keep warm.

Meanwhile, prepare the herbed mushrooms: In a medium-size bowl, combine all the ingredients for the mushrooms and toss until well coated. Grill the mushrooms, turning often, for 2 to 5 minutes, or until just beginning to soften.

To serve, divide the rice among serving plates and top with the mushrooms.

FRAGRANT RICE

½ medium-size onion

3 plum tomatoes

2 tablespoons olive oil

1½ cups basmati or Texmati rice

4 roasted garlic cloves (page 16), peeled & coarsely chopped

2 fresh sage leaves

1 imported bay leaf

½ teaspoon each cumin seeds & mustard seeds

½ teaspoon salt

3 cups chicken or vegetable broth

HERBED MUSHROOMS

1 portobello mushroom, stem removed, briefly rinsed & cut into ½-inch-thick slices

12 ounces shiitakes, creminis & button mushrooms, stems trimmed & briefly rinsed

¼ cup dry white wine

3 tablespoons olive oil

3 garlic cloves, finely chopped

2 teaspoons chopped fresh thyme

¼ teaspoon salt

¼ teaspoon freshly ground pepper

CHARRED ONIONS

Whole onions cook beautifully over the fire. Their outside layers turn a deep brown and the insides become soft and sweet. I like to serve them as an accompaniment to pork or beef, or as part of an appetizer platter with goat cheese, roasted garlic, grilled sweet bell peppers, and sourdough bread.

Serve 4 to 6

PREHEAT THE GRILL to medium and brush with oil.

Cut a 14-inch square of heavy-duty aluminum foil and fold the edges up to form a baking dish large enough to hold the onions in a single layer. Add the onions, drizzle the oil over them, and sprinkle with salt and pepper. Place the foil baking dish on the grill and grill the onions for 10 minutes. Using tongs, place the onions directly on the grill and continue grilling for 5 to 10 minutes longer, or until the centers are tender when pierced with a small knife. Transfer the onions to a small serving platter, pour any accumulated juices from the foil baking pan over the onions, and serve while hot.

6 small Vidalia, Walla Walla,
   or red onions, peeled
1 tablespoon olive oil

Salt & freshly ground pepper

WITH CASCABEL SAUCE

PORTOBELLOS

Serves 4

Cascabels are small round reddish-brown chiles. Here, their smoky, woodsy flavor is the perfect complement to the deep rich sweetness of the sun-dried tomatoes in the sauce. Served over grilled portobello mushrooms, it's a sublime combination.

PREHEAT THE GRILL to medium and brush with oil.

Grill the tomatoes, turning often, for 8 to 10 minutes, or until the skins are blistered and blackened, and the tomatoes are beginning to soften. Remove and set aside.

In a small dry skillet, pan-roast the chiles over medium-low heat, turning them often, for about 2 minutes, or until browned on all sides, watching to make sure that the chiles do not blacken or burn. When cool enough to handle, remove the stems and seeds.

Transfer the chiles to a small saucepan, and add the sun-dried tomatoes and the water. Bring to a boil over high heat, then remove from the heat.

In a food processor or blender, process the tomatoes, sun-dried tomatoes, the chiles, with their liquid, and the salt, until smooth. Press the sauce through a strainer into a small saucepan. Keep warm.

Brush the mushrooms with the oil and season with salt and pepper. Grill for 3 to 4 minutes, or until they begin to soften. Turn over and grill for about 2 minutes longer, or until the mushrooms are just tender.

Cut the mushrooms into ½-inch-thick slices and place on small plates. Garnish with the watercress sprigs, if using, and serve accompanied by the sauce.

CASCABEL & SUN-DRIED TOMATO SAUCE

2 plum tomatoes

5 dried cascabel chiles, cored & seeded

5 oil-packed sun-dried tomatoes, chopped

1 cup cold water

⅛ teaspoon salt

4 portobello mushrooms (4 to 6 inches in diameter)

¼ cup olive oil

Salt & freshly ground pepper

Watercress sprigs, for garnish (optional)

Serves 4

PREHEAT THE GRILL to medium and brush with oil.

Prepare the jalapeño dressing: In a small bowl, whisk together the lime juice, vinegar, jalapeño, garlic, salt, and pepper. Gradually add the oil in a slow stream, whisking until well combined. Set aside.

Brush the cut side of the tomatoes with the oil and season with salt and pepper. Grill the tomatoes, cut side down, for 1 to 1½ minutes, just until nicely marked but not softened. Remove to a warm plate.

Grill the mozzarella slices, on one side only, for about 10 to 15 seconds, just until nicely marked. Use a metal spatula to remove the mozzarella slices to the baking sheet, placing them grilled side up.

To serve, divide the mesclun salad among serving plates. Put 2 or 3 slices of the mozzarella on top of each serving and place 2 tomato halves alongside. Briefly whisk the dressing, drizzle over the salad, and sprinkle with cilantro leaves.

Grilled tomatoes do not have to be served warm. I find that they retain their slightly smoky flavor even after they have cooled. Either way, they are irresistible when paired with fresh mozzarella and enlivened with this fresh lime and jalapeño dressing.

JALAPEÑO DRESSING

- **3 tablespoons fresh lime juice**
- **1 tablespoon cider vinegar**
- **1 jalapeño chile, seeded & finely chopped**
- **1 garlic clove, minced**
- **¼ teaspoon salt**
- **¼ teaspoon freshly ground pepper**
- **3 tablespoons olive oil**

- **4 ripe yellow or red plum tomatoes, halved**
- **1 tablespoon olive oil**
- **Salt & freshly ground pepper**
- **2 balls fresh mozzarella cheese (4 to 6 ounces each), cut into ½-inch-thick slices**
- **5 cups loosely packed mesclun salad, washed & dried (about 4 ounces)**
- **Fresh cilantro leaves, for garnish**

GRILLED SQUASH SALAD

Serves 4

Calabasa, also known as Mexican squash, is a variety of summer squash with a taste similar to zucchini. Here in New Mexico, they are plentiful almost all summer long. If calabasas aren't available in your area, substitute any favorite summer squash.

PREHEAT THE GRILL to medium and brush with oil.

In a large bowl, put the calabasa, yellow squash, zucchini, and onion. In a small bowl, whisk together the oil, 1 tablespoon of the vinegar, the garlic, cumin, and ⅛ teaspoon salt. Add to the vegetables, tossing until evenly coated.

Grill all the squash and the onion for 2 to 3 minutes on each side, or until nicely marked and just beginning to soften. Remove the vegetables to a cutting board and set aside until cool enough to handle.

Cut the squash and onion crosswise into 1-inch pieces and put into a large bowl. Add the New Mexico chile, poblano chile, parsley, and thyme. Drizzle the remaining 1 tablespoon vinegar over the vegetables, season with salt and pepper, and toss gently to combine. Serve warm or at room temperature.

1 small calabasa quartered & cut crosswise into ¼-inch-thick slices or 4 patty pan squash (about 8 ounces), cut lengthwise into ¼-inch-thick slices

1 medium-size yellow squash, cut lengthwise into ¼-inch-thick slices

2 small zucchini, cut lengthwise into ¼-inch-thick slices

½ medium-size red onion, cut into ½-inch-thick slices

2 tablespoons olive oil

2 tablespoons balsamic vinegar

2 garlic cloves, minced

¼ teaspoon ground cumin

Salt & freshly ground pepper

1 New Mexico green chile, grilled, peeled, cored, seeded & coarsely chopped (page 24)

1 poblano chile, grilled, peeled, cored, seeded & cut into ¼-inch-wide strips (page 24)

3 tablespoons chopped fresh parsley

1 teaspoon finely chopped fresh thyme

Serves 4

If freshly made ravioli is not available, use the frozen variety. For the most flavor, serve this pasta salad warm or at room temperature, rather than chilled. As a variation, try the smoky sweet grilled tomato vinaigrette over spaghetti that has been tossed with lots of chopped fresh herbs.

PREHEAT THE GRILL to medium and brush with oil.

Prepare the grilled tomato vinaigrette: Grill the tomatoes, skin side down, for 3 to 5 minutes, or until softened. Remove. In a food processor, combine the grilled tomatoes, sun-dried tomatoes, garlic, vinegar, sugar, salt, and pepper. With the machine running, add the oils in a slow, steady stream, processing until smooth. Set aside.

Grill the corn, turning often, for 5 to 6 minutes, or until browned in spots. Meanwhile, grill the zucchini, turning once, for 1 to 2 minutes, or until grill-marked and just beginning to soften. Remove the vegetables and set aside to cool.

Cook the ravioli in a large pot of boiling water according to the package directions.

Meanwhile, using a sharp knife, cut the corn kernels from the cob and set aside. Stack a few of the slices of zucchini and cut lengthwise into ¼-inch-wide strips, then crosswise into 2-inch lengths. Repeat with the remaining zucchini.

Drain the ravioli and transfer to a large skillet. Add the corn, zucchini, black beans, scallions, cilantro, parsley, and tomato vinaigrette and stir gently, over low heat until heated through. Season with salt and pepper, gently toss, and serve.

GRILLED TOMATO VINAIGRETTE

2 plum tomatoes, halved

1 tablespoon chopped oil-packed sun-dried tomatoes

1 garlic clove, minced

⅓ cup balsamic vinegar

1 teaspoon packed brown sugar

¼ teaspoon salt

¼ teaspoon freshly ground pepper

⅓ cup vegetable oil

¼ cup olive oil

1 ear fresh corn, husk & silk removed

2 small zucchini, cut lengthwise into ¼-inch-thick slices

Two 9-ounce packages fresh or frozen ravioli (filled with black beans & chiles, or another variety)

1 cup cooked black beans, drained & rinsed if canned

2 scallions, chopped

3 tablespoons chopped fresh cilantro

2 tablespoons chopped fresh parsley

Salt & freshly ground pepper

Serves 4 to 6

Pinto beans have been a part of southwest cooking for a very long time. One trick to achieving tenderness and digestibility is to soak the beans overnight. Also, simmer the beans gently, and add salt only after the beans have become tender, since salt tends to toughen their skin.

IN A LARGE BOWL, soak the beans overnight in water to cover by 3 inches. Drain the beans, rinse well, and drain again.

Preheat the grill to medium and brush with oil.

Grill the tomatoes, turning them, for 8 to 10 minutes, or until blackened and slightly softened. Remove and let cool, then chop.

In a large saucepan, combine the beans and water and bring to a boil over medium heat. Using a slotted spoon, skim off any foam that rises to the surface. Reduce the heat to low and stir in the beer, tomatoes, garlic, and bay leaf. Cook, partially covered, for about 1½ hours, or until the beans are tender, adding water as necessary to keep the beans covered by ½ inch. Remove from the heat.

In a large skillet, heat the oil over medium heat until hot. Add the onion and cook, stirring, for 2 to 3 minutes, or until soft and translucent. Add the beans, with their cooking liquid, the chile powder, and salt, stirring to mix well. Reduce the heat to low and simmer, uncovered, for 15 to 20 minutes, or until the mixture thickens. Serve hot.

---

2 cups dried pinto beans (12 ounces), picked over & rinsed

4 plum tomatoes

6 cups cold water

One 12-ounce bottle dark Mexican beer, such as Negro Modelo or Dos Equis

3 garlic cloves, coarsely chopped

1 imported bay leaf

2 tablespoons olive oil

1 medium-size onion, chopped

2 tablespoons mild pure chile powder

½ teaspoon salt, or more to taste

Grilled chunks of crusty bread and vine-ripened tomatoes are the base for this red chile–spiked bread salad. Grilling the bread adds crunchiness, and the grilled tomatoes impart a delicious smoky quality.

PREHEAT THE GRILL to medium-hot and brush with oil.

Prepare the cumin vinaigrette: In a small skillet, heat 1 tablespoon of the oil over medium heat. Add the garlic, coarsely ground chiles, and cumin. Cook, stirring, for 1 minute, or until the garlic has softened and the cumin is fragrant. Transfer to a small bowl. Add the wine to the skillet and return to the heat. Cook, scraping the bottom of the pan with a wooden spoon to loosen any brown bits. Pour into the garlic mixture. Whisk in the remaining 4 tablespoons oil, vinegar, and lemon juice, whisking until blended. Set aside.

Grill the bread for 2 to 3 minutes on each side, or until golden. Cut into cubes, put into a large serving bowl, and set aside.

Brush the tomatoes with the oil. Grill for 1 to 2 minutes on each side, or until lightly marked. Cut into ¾-inch chunks and add to the bread, along with the olives, basil, parsley, and oregano.

Briefly whisk the dressing, pour over the panzanella salad, and toss until well mixed. Season with salt and pepper, toss again, and serve immediately.

CUMIN VINAIGRETTE
- 5 tablespoons olive oil
- 3 garlic cloves, chopped
- 2 teaspoons coarsely ground mild or hot pure chiles
- 1 teaspoon cumin seeds
- ¼ cup dry white wine
- 3 tablespoons each red wine vinegar & fresh lemon juice

- Four ¾-inch-thick large slices crusty bread
- 1 pound plum tomatoes, halved
- 12 Spanish green olives
- 2 tablespoons each coarsely chopped fresh basil & fresh parsley
- 2 teaspoons chopped fresh oregano
- Salt & freshly ground pepper

CUMIN-ORANGE BEAN SALAD

Serves 6

Grilling the tomatoes and red onion and pan toasting the cumin seeds brings rich flavor to this bean salad, making it the perfect side dish for grilled beef, pork, poultry, or seafood.

PREHEAT THE GRILL to medium-hot and brush with oil.

Prepare the cumin seed vinaigrette: Toast the cumin seeds in a small skillet over medium heat for about 2 minutes, or until lightly browned and fragrant. Transfer to a spice grinder or mortar and pestle and pound or grind, until slightly crushed but with some seeds left whole. Transfer to a small bowl and add the balsamic and wine vinegars, coarsely ground chiles, and orange zest. Gradually add the oil, whisking until blended. Set aside.

Grill the tomatoes and onion, turning once, for 3 to 4 minutes, or until the tomatoes are somewhat blackened but firm and the onion is beginning to brown. Remove from the grill and set aside until cool enough to handle.

Chop the vegetables into ½-inch pieces and put into a medium-size bowl. Add the beans, parsley, rosemary, capers, salt, and pepper. Briefly whisk the vinaigrette and pour over the bean salad, mixing well to combine. Cover and refrigerate until ready to serve. (This salad may be prepared up to 1 day ahead.)

TOASTED CUMIN SEED VINAIGRETTE

1½ teaspoons cumin seeds

3 tablespoons balsamic vinegar

2 tablespoons red wine vinegar

1 teaspoon coarsely ground medium-hot pure chiles

1 teaspoon grated orange zest

⅓ cup extra-virgin olive oil

3 plum tomatoes, halved

½ medium-size red onion

3 cups cooked small white beans, drained & rinsed if canned

1 cup cooked small red beans, drained & rinsed if canned

¼ cup chopped fresh parsley

2 teaspoons chopped fresh rosemary

2 teaspoons capers

½ teaspoon salt

½ teaspoon freshly ground pepper

LEMON-OREGANO POTATOES

Serves 6

I think it's the contrast of the earthy grilled flavor of the potatoes and the lightness of the lemon that makes these potatoes so special. Although the recipe gives a specific grilling time, grill them the way you like—sometimes I like them almost completely charred.

PREHEAT THE GRILL to medium and brush with oil.

In a large pot, cover the potatoes with water and bring to a boil over medium-high heat. Reduce the heat to medium-low and cook for 12 to 14 minutes, or until barely tender. Drain and transfer to a large bowl.

In a small bowl, whisk together 3 tablespoons of the lemon juice, the oil, 2 teaspoons of the oregano, the salt, and pepper. Pour over the potatoes, tossing until coated.

Grill the potatoes, cut side down, for 3 to 4 minutes, or until nicely marked. Turn the potatoes over and grill for 3 to 4 minutes longer, or until the skins are brown and crispy and the potatoes are tender when pierced with a fork. Return the potatoes to the bowl. Sprinkle with the remaining 2 tablespoons lemon juice, the parsley, and the remaining 1 teaspoon oregano, tossing until well mixed. Transfer to a serving dish and serve hot.

- 2 pounds small Yukon Gold potatoes, scrubbed & halved
- 5 tablespoons fresh lemon juice
- 2 tablespoons olive oil
- 1 tablespoon chopped fresh oregano
- ¼ teaspoon salt
- ¼ teaspoon freshly ground pepper
- 1 tablespoon chopped fresh parsley

GRILLED POTATOES

The first time I used dried chipotles, I was doubtful that they could be as smoky and hot as the ones packed in adobo sauce. But I was wrong, the flavor dried chipotles release when rehydrated is just as powerful and irresistible.

PREHEAT THE GRILL to medium and brush with oil.

Prepare the chipotle rub: Put all the chipotle rub ingredients in a spice grinder or mortar and pestle and pound or grind until finely ground. Set aside.

Cut the potatoes lengthwise in half. Cut each half lengthwise into 3 wedges, then cut crosswise in half. Put the russet and sweet potatoes into separate medium-size saucepans, cover with water, and bring to a boil over medium-high heat. Cook for 10 to 14 minutes, or until almost tender when pierced with a fork. Drain, then transfer to a large bowl. Add the chipotle rub and garlic, tossing until the potatoes are evenly coated.

Meanwhile, toast the cumin seeds in a small skillet over medium-low heat, stirring often, for about 2 minutes, or until fragrant. Transfer to a small dish and set aside.

Place the potatoes on the grill, cut side down, and grill, turning several times, for 4 to 6 minutes, or until nicely marked and very hot. Remove the potatoes to a serving dish. Sprinkle the lemon juice, cilantro, and cumin seeds over the potatoes, tossing until mixed well. Serve hot.

CHIPOTLE RUB

3 dried chipotle chiles

1 teaspoon mild pure chile powder

½ teaspoon salt

¼ teaspoon freshly ground pepper

2 sweet potatoes (about 8 ounces each), scrubbed

2 russet potatoes (about 8 ounces each), scrubbed

3 garlic cloves, minced

½ teaspoon cumin seeds

3 tablespoons fresh lemon juice

1 tablespoon chopped fresh cilantro

GRILLED VEGETABLE

Serves 4

The first time I tasted grilled carrots, I fell in love with their sweet roasted flavor. This simple couscous side dish with grilled carrots, smoky chiles, and sweet raisins, goes particularly well with grilled lamb skewers.

PREHEAT THE GRILL to medium and brush with oil.

In a small saucepan, bring the water to a boil. Add the couscous, cover tightly, and remove from the heat. Let stand for about 10 minutes, then fluff with a fork. Cover and set aside.

Grill the carrots, chiles, and onion, turning occasionally, for 3 to 4 minutes, or until the carrots are blackened and slightly wrinkled, the chiles are blistered and brown, and the onion is browned in spots and beginning to soften. Remove from the grill. When cool enough to handle, chop all the vegetables into ¼-inch pieces.

In a serving bowl, combine the couscous, grilled vegetables, parsley, raisins, and oil, tossing until well mixed. Season with salt and pepper and serve.

1 cup cold water
½ cup couscous
2 carrots, halved lengthwise
1 poblano chile, halved, cored, seeded, & ribs removed
1 Anaheim chile, halved, cored, seeded & ribs removed

½ medium-size red onion
¼ cup chopped fresh parsley
2 tablespoons raisins
1 tablespoon olive oil
Salt & freshly ground pepper

TABBOULEH

Serves 4 to 6

This variation on the classic bulgur salad contains grilled ripe tomatoes, crisp red bell pepper, and the heat of pure chile powder. The fresh parsley, mint, and oregano provide bright flavor accents. Serve this tabbouleh alongside grilled snapper, skewered chicken, or grilled vegetables.

PREHEAT THE GRILL to medium and brush with oil. Meanwhile, toast the sesame seeds in a small skillet over medium heat for about 2 minutes, or until golden. Transfer to a small dish and set aside.

In a medium-size bowl, pour the boiling water over the bulgur. Let stand for 30 minutes, or until all the water is absorbed. Fluff the bulgur with a fork and set aside.

Grill the tomatoes and bell pepper, turning often, for 4 to 6 minutes, or until slightly softened and the skins are blistered and brown. Remove and set aside to cool.

Cut the tomatoes and bell pepper into ½-inch dice and put into a large bowl. Add the bulgur, parsley, mint, oregano, chile powder, coarsely ground chiles, cumin, and sesame seeds, tossing until combined. Drizzle the lemon juice and olive oil over the salad, tossing until well blended. Season with salt and pepper, toss again, and serve.

2 tablespoons sesame seeds

1 cup boiling water

1 cup fine-grain bulgur

2 plum tomatoes

1 medium-size red bell pepper, halved, cored & seeded

1 cup chopped fresh parsley

¼ cup chopped fresh mint

2 teaspoons chopped fresh oregano

1 teaspoon mild or medium-hot pure chile powder

1 teaspoon coarsely ground mild or medium-hot pure chiles

½ teaspoon ground cumin

3 tablespoons fresh lemon juice

2 tablespoons olive oil

Salt & freshly ground pepper

DESSERTS

GRILLED CORNBREAD

Serves 8

When lightly grilled, this golden corn bread develops a pleasant crunch that pairs perfectly with the sweet strawberries and juicy blackberries.

PREHEAT THE OVEN TO 375°F. Grease a 9-x-5-inch loaf pan.

Prepare the corn bread: In a large bowl, combine the flour, cornmeal, sugar, baking powder, and salt, whisking until mixed. In a medium-size bowl, lightly beat the eggs. Add the buttermilk and melted butter, stirring until mixed. Pour over the dry ingredients, stirring with a rubber spatula just until blended. Pour into the prepared pan and sprinkle the cinnamon sugar over the top.

Bake for 35 to 40 minutes, or until the corn bread begins to pull away from the sides of the pan and a toothpick inserted into the center comes out clean. Let the corn bread cool in the pan on a wire rack for 10 minutes. Remove from the pan and cool completely on the wire rack.

Preheat the grill to medium and brush with oil.

Prepare the berry topping: In a large bowl, combine all the topping ingredients, tossing gently. Set aside until ready to serve.

Using a serrated knife, cut the corn bread into ½-thick slices. Grill for 30 to 45 seconds on each side, or until lightly toasted. Transfer the corn bread to dessert plates, spoon the berry topping over, and top with whipped cream.

CORN BREAD

1 cup all-purpose flour

1 cup yellow cornmeal

⅔ cup sugar

1 teaspoon baking powder

½ teaspoon salt

2 large eggs

1 cup buttermilk

5 tablespoons unsalted butter, melted & cooled

Cinnamon sugar (2 teaspoons sugar mixed with ¾ teaspoon ground cinnamon)

BERRY TOPPING

2 pints strawberries, hulled & thickly sliced

2 half-pints blackberries

½ cup fresh orange juice

2 tablespoons Triple Sec

⅛ teaspoon ground cinnamon

Sweetened whipped cream

MESQUITE HONEY

Mesquite honey is a caramel-colored honey with a slightly spicy, almost pungent flavor. Like the mesquite tree, it is quite common throughout Texas, central New Mexico, and southern Arizona. Mesquite honey is available through mail-order sources and in specialty food stores.

Serves 6

PREHEAT THE GRILL to medium and brush with oil.

Put the honey, cinnamon, and chile powder into a small bowl, stirring until well combined. Set aside.

Grill the figs, cut side down, for 1 to 2 minutes, or until nicely marked and warm. Turn the figs over and grill on the second side for about 30 seconds, just until warmed.

Place 3 fig halves, cut side up, on each serving plate. Drizzle the spiced honey over the figs onto the plates, creating a web-like pattern. Sprinkle with the pistachios, if using, and serve immediately.

½ cup mesquite or other
   fragrant honey
¼ teaspoon ground cinnamon
¼ teaspoon mild pure chile
   powder

9 large ripe figs, halved
3 tablespoons chopped
   pistachios (optional)

BUTTERMILK & LIME

Serves 4

The distinctively tangy taste of buttermilk, accented by pungent lime juice and balanced with a simple sugar syrup, makes a spectacular sherbet. Though low in calories, buttermilk makes a surprisingly rich sherbet with a truly satisfying creaminess, the perfect foil for the rich syrupy sweetness of the grilled pineapple.

PREPARE THE BUTTERMILK SHERBET: In a small saucepan, combine the water and sugar and bring to a boil over medium-high heat. Reduce the heat to medium and boil for 1 to 2 minutes, or until the sugar has dissolved, brushing down any sugar crystals from the sides of the pan with a pastry brush dipped in cold water. Set the pan over a bowl of ice water and cool the sugar syrup to room temperature, stirring occasionally. Stir the lime juice, corn syrup, lime zest, and mint into the sugar syrup.

In a medium-size bowl, whisk together the buttermilk and sugar syrup. Pour into an ice cream maker and freeze according to the manufacturer's instructions. Transfer to a covered container and place in the freezer.

Preheat the grill to medium and brush with oil.

Grill the pineapple slices for 1 to 2 minutes on each side, or until grill-marked. Place the warm pineapple slices on dessert plates, top each serving with a scoop of the sherbet, and garnish with mint sprigs if using.

BUTTERMILK SHERBET

½ cup cold water

½ cup sugar

¼ cup plus 2 tablespoons fresh lime juice

2 tablespoons light corn syrup

1 tablespoon plus 1 teaspoon grated lime zest

2 to 3 teaspoons finely chopped fresh mint

2 cups buttermilk

Four 1-inch-thick slices ripe pineapple

Fresh mint sprigs, for garnish (optional)

NOTE: The sherbet is best if eaten within 2 days.

Grilling slices of angel food cake takes only a few seconds. Warming the peaches and apricots is quick too. The result is an elegant dessert, beautiful to look at and delightful to eat.

Serves 8

PREHEAT THE GRILL to medium and brush with oil.

Prepare the raspberry sauce: In a blender or food processor, combine the raspberries, confectioners' sugar, and orange juice, processing until smooth. Press through a fine-mesh strainer into a small bowl, cover, and refrigerate.

Put the peaches and apricots into a medium-size bowl. Add the rum and brown sugar, gently tossing to coat.

Grill the fruit, turning once, for 30 to 45 seconds, or until lightly grill-marked but not mushy. Remove and keep warm. Grill the cake slices for 10 to 15 seconds on each side, or until nicely marked and golden.

To serve, spoon a small amount of raspberry sauce onto each serving plate. Place the slices of cake on top of the sauce and spoon the fruit and any accumulated juices on top. Garnish with mint sprigs, if desired, and serve.

RASPBERRY SAUCE

2 half-pints fresh raspberries or one 12-ounce package frozen raspberries, thawed

3 tablespoons confectioners' sugar

3 tablespoons fresh orange juice

4 ripe peaches, halved, pitted &each cut into 8 wedges

4 ripe apricots, halved & pitted

2 tablespoons dark rum (optional)

1 tablespoon packed light brown sugar

One store-bought 10-ounce loaf angel food cake or pound cake, cut into ¾-inch-thick slices

Fresh mint sprigs, for garnish (optional)

NOTE: Leftover raspberry sauce can be refrigerated for up to 1 week or frozen for up to 1 month.

GRILLED PEACH GRANITA

Serves 6

P REHEAT THE GRILL to medium and brush with oil.

Grill the peaches, turning them, for 3 to 4 minutes, or until grill-marked and tender. Remove and when cool enough to handle, peel and coarsely chop.

Transfer the peaches to a food processor or blender and process until smooth. Add the water, juice concentrate, lemon juice, coriander, and chile powder. Process, pulsing once or twice, just until well combined. Pour the mixture into a shallow glass or ceramic baking dish approximately 9 inches square. Cover tightly with aluminum foil and freeze for at least 4 hours, or until the granita is completely frozen. (The granita can be made up to 3 days ahead.)

To serve, use a metal spoon to scrape across the surface of the granita, transferring the ice shards to chilled dessert glasses or wine goblets, without packing them. Garnish with mint sprigs, if using, and serve immediately.

The word granita is derived from the Italian word for grainy. It describes flavored ices made without stirring (or churning in an ice cream maker), unlike most ices and ice creams. In this unusual version, grilled peaches and just a hint of red chile powder are combined to create a refreshing dessert with a unique taste.

1½ pounds ripe peaches, halved, pitted & cut into ½-inch-thick slices	2 tablespoons fresh lemon juice
1 cup cold water	¾ teaspoon ground coriander
¾ cup frozen white grape and peach juice concentrate, thawed	⅛ teaspoon hot pure chile powder
	Fresh mint sprigs, for garnish (optional)

PEAR PARFAIT

SPICED

When the syrupy juice of ripe pears mingles with brown sugar, vanilla, and spices, the result is a decadent caramel sauce. Layered with vanilla ice milk and topped with a sprinkling of pistachios, this luscious dessert can compete with any hot fudge sundae.

Serves 4

PREHEAT THE GRILL to medium and brush with oil.

In a small bowl, mix together the brown sugar, cinnamon, allspice, and vanilla. Add the pears and toss until evenly coated. Let sit for 5 to 10 minutes.

Use a slotted spoon to remove the pears from the bowl, reserving the accumulated juices in the bowl. Grill the pears, cut side down, for 4 to 6 minutes, or until the brown sugar glaze turns a rich brown. Remove the pears to a cutting board and cut into 1/2-inch chunks. Return the pears to the reserved juices and toss to coat. Set aside to cool to room temperature.

To serve, alternate layers of the pears and ice milk into chilled dessert glasses or wine goblets, beginning and ending with the pears. Drizzle 2 to 3 teaspoons of maple syrup on top of the sundaes, if desired, and garnish with the pistachios. Serve immediately.

2 tablespoons packed brown sugar

¼ teaspoon ground cinnamon

Pinch of ground allspice

½ teaspoon vanilla extract

2 firm but ripe red Bartlett, D'Anjou, or Bosc pears, halved & cored

1 quart vanilla ice milk

2 to 3 tablespoons maple syrup (optional)

2 tablespoons chopped unsalted pistachio nuts

WITH MANGO SAUCE

BANANAS

Grilling slightly caramelizes the sugar in the bananas, producing a rich bittersweet flavor. This is a perfect dessert to follow a meal of grilled fish, rice, and fruit salsa.

PREHEAT THE GRILL to medium and brush with oil.

In a food processor or blender, puree the mango until smooth. Transfer the sauce to a plastic squirt bottle or a small pitcher. Set aside.

In a small saucepan, melt the butter over medium heat. Reduce the heat to low and add the sugar and rum, stirring until smooth and the sugar has dissolved. Put the bananas into a shallow dish. Brush the rum butter mixture on both sides of the bananas.

Grill the bananas, cut side down, for about 45 seconds, or just until nicely marked. Carefully turn and continue to grill for another 30 seconds, or until hot. Remove to a cutting board.

Cut the bananas crosswise in half. Squirt or pour about 3 tablespoons of the mango sauce onto each serving plate. Divide the bananas among the plates and serve.

1 large ripe mango, peeled, pitted & cut into chunks, or one 10-ounce jar sliced mango, drained

1 tablespoon unsalted butter

2 teaspoons packed brown sugar

2 tablespoons dark rum

4 firm but ripe bananas, peeled & halved lengthwise

SALSAS, RUBS & MARINADES

DE GALLO

PICO

This salsa, Mexico's most common condiment, is eaten with everything from eggs and beans to tortilla chips to potatoes to shellfish and poultry. Here in the Southwest it has become very popular too, simply because pico de gallo tastes so good with everything.

Makes about 2 cups

PREHEAT THE GRILL to medium and brush with oil.

Grill the jalapeños, turning often, for about 2 minutes, or until the skins are blistered and brown. Remove from the grill and when cool enough to handle, halve, seed, and remove the ribs. Finely chop the jalapeños and put into a small bowl. Stir in the remaining ingredients and let sit for 1 hour to allow the flavors to blend.

4 jalapeño chiles
2 plum tomatoes, chopped
½ cup chopped onions
¼ cup chopped fresh cilantro

3 tablespoons white vinegar
2 tablespoons water
1 tablespoon vegetable oil
¼ teaspoon salt

NOTE: This salsa tastes best eaten the day it is prepared, but it will keep for up to 2 days, tightly covered in the refrigerator.

Makes 1½ cups

PREHEAT THE GRILL TO MEDIUM.

Grill the jalapeños for 2 to 3 minutes, or until the skins are blistered and brown. Remove from the grill and when cool enough to handle, halve, seed, and finely chop.

Put the jalapeños into a small bowl, add the remaining ingredients, and stir until well combined. Serve freshly made, or cover and refrigerate for up to 3 hours.

Salsa fresca, like pico de gallo, is a common Mexican salsa, now found on tables all over the Southwest. Salsa fresca is less fiery than pico de gallo, since it contains more tomatoes and fewer jalapeños.

2 jalapeño chiles

4 plum tomatoes, cut into ¼-inch dice

¼ cup fresh lime juice

3 garlic cloves, minced

2 tablespoons finely chopped fresh cilantro

1 tablespoon olive oil

¼ teaspoon salt

TOMATO-CHIPOTLE SALSA

Makes 2 cups

Mark Miller's Coyote Cafe serves and sells a fire-roasted salsa that is similar to this one. After tasting this version, you'll understand its popularity. It is both sweet, from the tomatoes, and hot, from the smoky chipotles. Besides its role as an appetizer served with chips, this salsa makes an excellent topping for grilled beef, fish, or pork.

PREHEAT THE GRILL to medium and brush with oil.

Grill the onion, turning occasionally, for 6 to 8 minutes, or until blackened in spots and almost tender when pierced in the center with a small knife. Meanwhile, grill the tomatoes, turning often, for 3 to 4 minutes, or until the skins are blistered and brown. Remove the vegetables from the grill and when cool enough to handle, coarsely chop.

In a food processor or blender, combine the tomatoes and onion, garlic, chipotle chiles, adobo sauce, oil, cumin, and salt. Process, pulsing 3 or 4 times, until the mixture forms a chunky puree. Transfer the salsa to a serving bowl and stir in the cilantro. Store the salsa, covered, in the refrigerator, until ready to serve.

½ medium-size onion

6 plum tomatoes

4 roasted garlic cloves (page 16), peeled

4 chipotle chiles packed in adobo sauce

1 tablespoon adobo sauce (from chipotle chiles)

2 tablespoons olive oil

½ teaspoon ground cumin

½ teaspoon salt

2 tablespoons chopped fresh cilantro

NOTE: This salsa will keep, tightly covered, in the refrigerator for 3 to 5 days.

Makes 2 cups

PREHEAT THE GRILL TO medium and brush with oil.

In a medium-size bowl, pour the boiling water over the pastilla and ancho chiles. Set aside for 15 to 20 minutes, or until softened.

Grill the onion, turning occasionally, for 6 to 8 minutes, or until blackened in spots and almost tender when pierced in the center with a small knife. Meanwhile, grill the tomatoes, turning often, for 3 to 4 minutes, or until the skins are blistered and brown. Remove the vegetables from the grill and when cool enough to handle, coarsely chop.

In a food processor or blender, process the chiles with their liquid until smooth. Press the chiles through a strainer into a medium-size bowl, pressing on the solids with the back of a wooden spoon.

Finely chop the tomatoes and onion. Add to the bowl along with the garlic, vinegar, cilantro, and salt, stirring well to combine. Cover and refrigerate until ready to serve.

Anchos and pasillas are two of the most commonly used dried chiles in Mexico. Both are described as having a mild fruity flavor with coffee and licorice undertones. To me, the chiles offer a dark richness that complements the flavor of grilled tomatoes to make a truly memorable salsa—one that is a great accompaniment to grilled beef, seafood, pork, or chicken.

1 cup boiling water
2 pasilla chiles
2 ancho chiles
½ medium-size red onion
4 plum tomatoes

5 roasted garlic cloves (page 16), peeled & chopped
3 tablespoons cider vinegar
3 tablespoons chopped fresh cilantro
¾ teaspoon salt

NOTE: Red chile salsa will keep, tightly covered, in the refrigerator for up to 1 week.

CHILE-PINEAPPLE

Makes 2 cups

PREHEAT THE GRILL TO medium and brush with oil.

Grill the onion, turning several times, for 3 to 4 minutes, or until beginning to brown but still firm. Remove from the grill. Meanwhile, grill the pineapple slices for 1 to 1½ minutes on each side, or until nicely marked but still firm.

When the pineapple is cool enough to handle, use a small round cutter or corer to remove the core from each slice. Coarsely chop the pineapple and onion and put into a food processor. Pulse several times, or until the mixture forms a chunky puree.

Transfer to a large bowl and add the jalapeños, cilantro, garlic, vinegar, oil, and salt, mixing well. Cover and refrigerate until ready to serve. For the best flavor, allow the salsa to come to room temperature before serving. (Keeps up to 3 days in the refrigerator.)

In this recipe, the pineapple's sweetness is mellowed by grilling and the jalapeños provide just the right amount of heat. This versatile salsa goes wonderfully with everything from chips to chicken, pork chops, and even grilled fish.

½ medium-size red onion

1 medium-size pineapple (about 2 pounds), trimmed, peeled & cut crosswise into ¾-inch-thick slices

2 jalapeño chiles, seeded & chopped

2 tablespoons chopped fresh cilantro

2 garlic cloves, minced

2 tablespoons cider vinegar

1 tablespoon olive oil

½ teaspoon salt

CHILE SALSA

Traditionally, roasted New Mexico green chiles are used in sauces and stews, or as a condiment, rather than in fresh salsas. Here they are grilled and combined with traditional salsa ingredients to allow their full flavor to come through. Serve as an alternative to more traditional red salsas, accompanied by chips, or as a topping for grilled chicken or fish.

PREHEAT THE GRILL to medium and brush with oil.

Grill the chiles and onion, turning often, for 6 to 8 minutes, or until the chiles are blistered and brown but the flesh is not charred, and the onion is almost tender in the center when pierced with a small knife. Wrap the chiles in paper towels, seal in a plastic bag, and let steam for 10 minutes. Remove the chiles and cool.

Meanwhile, chop the onion. Put it into a medium-size bowl along with the tomatoes, garlic, cilantro, lime juice, and salt.

Carefully peel, core, and seed the chiles and remove the ribs. Cut the chiles into $\frac{1}{4}$-inch dice and add to the bowl, mixing well. Refrigerate the salsa, covered, until ready to serve.

6 mild, medium, or hot
   New Mexico green chiles

1 medium-size onion,
   quartered

4 plum tomatoes, chopped

2 garlic cloves, minced

2 tablespoons chopped
   fresh cilantro

$\frac{1}{4}$ cup fresh lime juice

$\frac{1}{2}$ teaspoon salt

NOTE: The flavor of green chile salsa is best the day it is made, but it will keep, tightly covered in the refrigerator, for 1 to 3 days.

Makes 2 cups

This fresh peach salsa is just sweet enough to balance the heat of the jalapeño perfectly. Serve it alongside grilled chicken or a mild flavored fish such as halibut.

PREHEAT THE GRILL TO medium-hot (see Note).

Grill the jalapeño for 2 to 3 minutes, or until the skin is blistered and brown. Set the jalapeño aside until cool, then cut into thin rings.

Put all the salsa ingredients in a small bowl and stir well to combine. Serve immediately.

1 red jalapeño chile

3 ripe peaches, peeled, halved, pitted & cut into ½-inch wedges

2 tablespoons fresh lime juice

1 tablespoon chopped fresh cilantro

1 tablespoon chopped onion

1 teaspoon olive oil

⅛ teaspoon salt

NOTE: It is not necessary to grill the jalpeño for this recipe, but if you are lighting your grill for another use, grilling the chile adds great roasted flavor to the salsa.

ORANGE RUB

Tamarind paste is made from the fleshy insides of tamarind tree pods. First the pods are boiled, and then the tangy black pulp is scraped out. In Mexico and the Caribbean, a refreshing drink is made from the tamarind paste, sugar, water, and ice. It is also used as a marinade base for rich meats such as pork and beef.

Makes 1 cup

PREHEAT THE GRILL to medium and brush with oil.

Grill the tomatoes, turning them, for 8 to 10 minutes, or until the skins are charred in spots and the tomatoes are almost tender. Remove from the grill, and when cool enough to handle, coarsely chop.

In a food processor or blender, combine the tomatoes and the remaining ingredients and process until a smooth thick paste forms. Transfer to a container and store in the refrigerator for up to 1 week.

2 plum tomatoes

3 tablespoons tamarind paste or concentrate*

Juice and grated zest of 1 orange (about ⅓ cup juice & 1 tablespoon zest)

2 chipotle chiles packed in adobo sauce

2 garlic cloves, chopped

1 tablespoon honey

2 teaspoons ground coriander

½ teaspoon ground cumin

½ teaspoon freshly ground pepper

*Tamarind paste can be found in Indian markets and some specialty food stores.

RED CHILE RUB

This is a basic rub, milder than those that contain chipotles, cayenne, or habanero chiles. Its mild hot-sweet flavor, with just a hint of cumin, makes it perfect for sprinkling over everything from vegetables to fish to beef.

Makes about ½ cup

COMBINE ALL THE INGREDIENTS in a spice grinder or mortar and pestle and process or pound until finely ground. Transfer to an airtight container and store at room temperature for up to 3 months.

⅓ cup mild pure chile powder

2 teaspoons dried oregano

2 teaspoons sugar

1 teaspoon kosher salt

¼ teaspoon ground cumin

¼ teaspoon freshly ground pepper

Makes about 1 cup

PREHEAT THE GRILL TO medium and brush with oil.

Grill the chile, turning several times, for 3 to 5 minutes, or until the skin is blistered and brown. Wrap the chile in a paper towel, seal in a plastic bag, and let steam for 10 minutes. Set aside to cool.

Meanwhile, toast the cumin seeds in a small skillet over medium-low heat for about 2 minutes, or until fragrant.

In a food processor or blender, combine the cumin seeds, garlic, vinegar, oregano, allspice, salt, and pepper. Process until a smooth paste forms. Transfer the paste to a small bowl or container.

Peel, stem, and seed the chile, and finely chop. Add the chile to the garlic paste, stirring until blended. Cover the dish tightly and store in the refrigerator for up to 5 days.

This wet rub is the perfect seasoning for larger cuts of meat such as steaks or pork chops. Just a thin layer of the rub will provide the right amount of seasoning. This rub tends to char easily when grilled, but that's okay. The slightly charred flavor, along with the allspice, gives the rub its authentic Mexican taste.

1 New Mexico mild or hot green chile	1 teaspoon dried oregano
½ teaspoon cumin seeds	⅛ teaspoon ground allspice
2 heads roasted garlic (page 16), peeled	½ teaspoon salt
1 tablespoon cider vinegar	½ teaspoon freshly ground pepper

OF CHILES

ADOBO SAUCE A smoky-flavored tomato-and-chile-based Mexican sauce used in salsas and marinades. Adobo sauce was originally a paste used to preserve strips of meat as they hung to air-dry. Canned chipotles are packed in adobo sauce.

ANAHEIM CHILE Similar in size, shape, and flavor to its close cousin the New Mexico green chile, this long, narrow, medium-size fresh green chile is commonly roasted or used in cooking, but is rarely eaten raw. Usually about 5 to 6 inches long, this mild chile has a less acidic, more vegetable-like flavor than the New Mexico green chile. The ripe red Anaheim is sweeter than the green.

ANCHO CHILE The ancho chile is the dried poblano chile, 3 to 4 inches wide at the top ("ancho" means wide in Spanish) and 5 inches long, tapering to a roundish end. It's color varies from dark winy red to almost brown and is mild to medium-hot with a slightly sweet, fruity, and woodsy flavor. It is often confused with the pasilla chile.

CASCABEL Cascabels are smooth, round, brownish-red dried chiles, approximately one to two inches in diameter. Cascabel means "rattle" in Spanish. These chiles were named for the rattling sound their seeds made in the dried shells. They have a dark tannic flavor and are medium-hot.

CHILE CARIBE These are medium to hot dried coarsely ground pure red chiles.The chile seeds are included for additional heat. They are a Southwestern version of crushed red pepper flakes, but are somwwhat hotter.

CHILE PÉQUIN Barely an inch long and light reddish-orange in color, these slightly oval-shaped, intensely hot chile péquins are most often used in their dried form. They are usually used to flavor sauces, marinades, and vinegars. Chile péquins are related to a variety of wild chile that is found in Mexico.

CHILE POWDER In this book, chile powder refers to pure finely ground dried New Mexico red chiles, whether mild, medium, or hot — not to blends of "chili" powder, which contain cumin, oregano, and other spices. Red chiles are also available as coarsely ground chiles. (See New Mexico red chile.)

CHIPOTLE CHILE Chipotles are smoked dried jalapeño chiles. They are 2 to 4 inches long and brownish in color. Often sold in small cans, packed in adobo sauce, chipotles have an unmistakable smoky flavor and are medium to hot. Chipotle chiles are also packaged in their dried form, both whole and ground.

HABANERO CHILE Ranging in color from green to yellow and orange to red, these 1 to 2 inch long lantern-shaped chiles are often cited as the hottest chiles in the world. They are available fresh and dried.

JALAPEÑO CHILE Jalapeños are perhaps the most widely available fresh chile. They are 2 to 3 inches long and about an inch in diameter at the stem end, with a smooth skin and thick flesh. They can vary in heat from medium to hot. Jalapeños are most often used when green and not fully ripe;. The bright-red ripe jalapeños are slightly sweeter than the green variety. Jalapeños are also available dried, ground, canned, and pickled. Dried and smoked they are known as chipotle chiles. They are versatile and can be added to just about any food to add a bit of heat.

NEW MEXICO GREEN CHILE These long 6 to 9 inch narrow, pale-to-darkish-green chiles vary in heat from mild to very hot. Their flavor has been described as weedy and acidic. Popular in southwestern cooking, they are almost never eaten raw, but instead are roasted and used in sauces, soups, stews, salsas, salads, and sandwiches, stuffed for chiles rellenos, or made into fillings for tacos, enchiladas, burritos, and tostadas. They are also available canned, dried, and frozen.

NEW MEXICO RED CHILE This is the ripe form of the New Mexico green chile, bright red when fresh and dark red to faded red-orange when dried. These are the chiles used to make ristras, the long chains of chiles used decoratively all over the Southwest. In cooking, they are used roasted and in their dried form (whole, crushed, or ground) and range in heat from mild to hot. They have an earthy acidic flavor.

PASILLA CHILE The dried pasilla is wrinkled and brown, about 5 to 6 inches long and an inch or so in diameter. In Spanish, pasilla means "little raisin", referring perhaps to both its appearance and sweet dark raisin-like flavor. Pasillas are dried chilaca chiles which are rarely used fresh; they range from mild to medium on the heat scale. (Pasillas are sometimes confused with ancho chiles, which are dried poblanos.)

POBLANO CHILE Poblano chiles are a greenish-black colored, medium- to thick-fleshed chiles about 3 to 4 inches wide and 4 to 5 inches long, with a pronounced pointed end. In Southwestern cooking they are rarely used raw, but are roasted or cooked and used in sauces, stews, soups, and salsas, much like the Anaheim and New Mexico green chiles. They vary in heat from mild to medium to hot and have an earthy, smoky flavor. In their dried form they are called ancho chiles.

SERRANO CHILE These are small intensely hot chiles, used fresh when still green or dried when allowed to ripen until red. Fresh serranos are bullet-shaped cylinders, about 1 to 3 inches long and less than 1/2 inch in diameter. Dried red serranos are available whole and in powdered form.

TO ROAST FRESH CHILES

To roast fresh chiles, put on a medium-hot grill (or directly over a gas flame or under the broiler) and grill, turning, for 2 to 6 minutes, or until the skins are completely blistered and brown but the flesh is not charred. Using tongs, remove from the grill. Wrap in a paper towel and put into a plastic bag for 10 minutes. Remove from the bag and let sit until cool enough to handle. Wearing rubber gloves, peel away the skin, using a small knife, and remove the core, seeds, and ribs if necessary. Roasted chiles can be refrigerated for up to 5 days or frozen for up to 3 months.

Not all fresh chiles should be roasted until their skins turn black. Those that have thinner flesh, like New Mexico green chiles and sometimes even Anaheims, should be roasted only until their skins blister and brown. Otherwise, the flesh will be burned. When pan-roasting dried chiles, watch them closely, turning them often. Be careful not to blacken their skins, as this would produce a bitter taste.

INDEX

CONVERSION TABLE

LENGTH

U.S. Measurements	Metrics
$1/8$ inch	3 mm
$1/4$ inch	6 mm
$3/8$ inch	1 cm
$1/2$ inch	1.2 cm
$3/4$ inch	2 cm
1 inch	2.5 cm
$1\,1/4$ inches	3.1 cm
$1\,1/2$ inches	3.7 cm
2 inches	5 cm
3 inches	7.5 cm
4 inches	10 cm
5 inches	12.5 cm

WEIGHTS

Ounces and Pounds	Metrics
$1/4$ ounce	7 grams
$1/3$ ounce	10 g
$1/2$ ounce	14 g
1 ounce	28 g
$1\,1/2$ ounces	42 g
$1\,1/4$ ounces	50 g
2 ounces	57 g
3 ounces	85 g
$3\,1/2$ ounces	100 g
4 ounces ($1/4$ pound)	114 g
6 ounces	170 g
8 ounces ($1/2$ pound)	227 g
9 ounces	250 g
16 ounces (1 pound)	464 g

LIQUID MEASURES

tsp.: teaspoon/Tbs.: tablespoon

Spoons and Cups	Metric Equivalents
$1/4$ tsp.	1.23 milliliters
$1/2$ tsp.	2.5 ml
$3/4$ tsp.	3.7 ml
1 tsp.	5 ml
1 dessertspoon	10 ml
1 Tbs. (3 tsp.)	15 ml
2 Tbs. (1 ounce)	30 ml
$1/4$ cup	60 ml
$1/3$ cup	80 ml
$1/2$ cup	120 ml
$2/3$ cup	160 ml
$3/4$ cup	180 ml
1 cup (8 ounces)	240 ml
2 cups (1 pint)	480 ml
3 cups	720 ml
4 cups (1 quart)	1 liter
4 quarts (1 gallon)	3.75 liters

TEMPERATURE

°F (Fahrenheit)		°C (Centigrade or Celsius)
32	(water freezes)	0
200		95
212	(water boils)	100
250		120
275		135
300	(slow oven)	150
325		160
350	(moderate oven)	175
375		190
400	(hot oven)	205
425		220
450	(very hot oven)	232
475		245
500	(extremely hot oven)	260

APPROXIMATE EQUIVALENTS

1 kilo is slightly more than 2 pounds
1 liter is slightly more than 1 quart
1 meter is slightly over 3 feet
1 centimeter is approximately $3/8$ inch